A CHILD'S INTRODUCTION TO
POETRY

A CHILD'S INTRODUCTION TO

POETRY

Listen While You Learn About the MAGIC WORDS That Have

MOVED MOUNTAINS, WON BATTLES, and Made Us LAUGH AND CRY

Michael Driscoll   Illustrated by Meredith Hamilton

BLACK DOG
& LEVENTHAL
PUBLISHERS
NEW YORK

Black Dog & Leventhal Publishers
Hachette Book Group
1290 Avenue of the Americas
New York, NY 10104

www.hachettebookgroup.com
www.blackdogandleventhal.com

Originally published in hardcover by Black Dog & Leventhal Publishers in 2003.

First revised edition: March 2020

Black Dog & Leventhal Publishers is an imprint of Perseus Books, LLC, a subsidiary of Hachette Book Group, Inc. The Black Dog & Leventhal Publishers name and logo are trademarks of Hachette Book Group, Inc.

The publisher is not responsible for websites (or their content) that are not owned by the publisher.

The Hachette Speakers Bureau provides a wide range of authors for speaking events. To find out more, go to www.HachetteSpeakersBureau.com or call (866) 376-6591.

Print book interior design by SJI Associates, Inc. and Carlos Esparza

LCCN: 2019934629
ISBNs: 978-0-7624-6910-9 (hardcover), 978-0-7624-6909-3 (ebook),
978-0-7624-6966-6 (ebook), 978-0-7624-6967-3 (ebook)

Printed in China

IM

10 9 8 7 6 5 4 3 2 1

CONTENTS

7
Introducing Professor Driscoll

PART ONE

THE RHYMES AND THEIR REASONS

PART TWO
POETRY'S GREATS
RULERS OF RHYME, LEGENDS OF THE LYRIC, AND SUPERSTARS OF THE SPOKEN WORD

Hey there! Welcome to the world of poetry, a fun and exciting place—sometimes sad, sometimes silly, sometimes scary—where anything can happen through the magic power of words.

I'm Professor Driscoll, and I'll be your guide as we listen and learn about what makes poetry so special.

You might think of poetry as the stuff that fills thick books on dusty shelves in dark libraries. But it's much more than that. Poetry can be found just about everywhere, from the words to your favorite song on the radio to the jingle from that commercial you can't get out of your head. We'll take a look at the many different types of poems and learn what makes each unique. Then we'll meet some of the greatest poets from around the world and throughout history, and discover what was so extraordinary about their poems.

On the way, we'll listen along as each poem comes to life. Go to **www.blackdogand-leventhal.com/ChildsIntroPoetry** to download 65 audio tracks. (When you see ➍ **PLAY TRACK,** you'll know it's time to play the poetry readings.) We'll learn the special words used by poets in the sections called "If You're a Poet, You Should Know It." Any tricky words within the poems will be explained in the sections called **"Words for the Wise."**

But don't worry about hard words. This isn't like one of your classes at school. It's sup-posed to be fun! Now, just to get you warmed up, we'll start with a poem by the legendary writer William Blake (more about him later). The poet compares himself to an entertainer playing music on a pipe and singing songs—much to the delight of his young listener. It's an example of just how great poetry can be.

INTRODUCTION TO

SONGS OF INNOCENCE AND OF EXPERIENCE

by William Blake

Piping down the valleys wild
Piping songs of pleasant glee
On a cloud I saw a child,
And he laughing said to me,

"Pipe a song about a Lamb";
So I piped with merry chear;
"Piper pipe that song again"—
So I piped, he wept to hear.

"Drop thy pipe thy happy pipe
Sing thy songs of happy chear";
So I sung the same again

While he wept with joy to hear.
"Piper sit thee down and write
In a book that all may read"—
So he vanish'd from my sight.
And I pluck'd a hollow reed,

And I made a rural pen,
And I stain'd the water clear,
And I wrote my happy songs
Every child may joy to hear.

 **PLAY TRACK 1**

PART ONE

The Rhymes and Their Reasons

NURSERY RHYMES

You may not remember it, but the first poem you ever heard was probably a **nursery rhyme**.

Some people think poetry is made strictly for brainy college students, stuffy old professors, and bored bookstore clerks. Not true! Poems can be enjoyed by everybody, and nursery rhymes are a great example.

These poems are usually brief, fun, and silly, with easy rhymes that just about anyone can follow. They often contain wacky images—like dogs wearing clothes and families living in shoes—a lot like goings-on in the cartoons you're used to watching.

The Legend of Mother Goose

Probably the most famous author of nursery rhymes is, you guessed it, Mother Goose. Some say a real "Mother Goose" lived in New England three hundred years ago. Others claim she was from France, and from many years earlier. No one knows for sure. A book of poems for children entitled *Mother Goose's Melody* was published in England in 1781, and the name "Mother Goose" has been associated with children's poetry ever since.

Higglety, Pigglety, Pop ➛ PLAY TRACK 2

Samuel Goodrich thought nursery rhymes were bad for kids. In 1846, he wrote "Higglety, Pigglety, Pop" as an example of how silly and worthless the poems were. Too bad for him—it's now a nursery-rhyme classic!

The Kite ➛ PLAY TRACK 3

This modern nursery rhyme describes the fantasy of every kid who's ever held on to a string and watched a kite dancing high in the sky.

Little Miss Muffet ➛ PLAY TRACK 4

The original "Little Miss Muffet" may have been the daughter of a famous sixteenth-century spider expert, Dr. Muffet. Or maybe not—no one knows for sure.

Twinkle, Twinkle, Little Star ➛ PLAY TRACK 5

"Twinkle, Twinkle, Little Star" is one of the most famous poems in the English language and was written by the British poet Jane Taylor in the early nineteenth century.

Hush-a-Bye, Baby ➛ PLAY TRACK 6

Some think "Hush-a-Bye, Baby" was written after early American settlers saw how Native Americans hung their babies' cradles from tree branches.

Higglety, Pigglety, Pop

Higglety, pigglety, pop!
The dog has eaten the mop;
    The pig's in a hurry,
    The cat's in a flurry,
Higglety, pigglety, pop!

—*Samuel Goodrich*

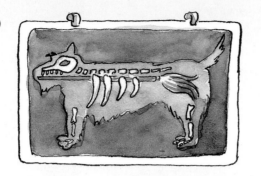

Twinkle, Twinkle, Little Star

Twinkle, Twinkle, little star,
How I wonder what you are!
Up above the world so high,
Like a diamond in the sky.

—*Jane Taylor*

The Kite

I often sit and wish that I
Could be a kite up in the sky,
And ride upon the breeze and go
Whichever way I chanced to blow.

Hush-a-Bye, Baby

Hush-a-bye, baby, on the tree top,
When the wind blows the cradle will rock;
When the **bough** breaks the cradle will fall,
Down will come baby, cradle, and all.

Little Miss Muffet

Little Miss Muffet
Sat on a **tuffet**,
Eating her **curds and whey**;
There came a big spider,
Who sat down beside her
And frightened Miss Muffet away.

There Was an Old Woman Who Lived in a Shoe

There was an old woman who lived in a shoe,
She had so many children she didn't know what to do;
She gave them some **broth** without any bread;
She whipped them all soundly and put them to bed.

There Was an Old Woman Who Lived in a Shoe
◆► PLAY TRACK 7

Elizabeth Vergoose lived in Boston in the late eighteenth century, and some think she was the real Mother Goose. She had six children and ten stepchildren (but we think she probably lived in a house).

Words for the Wise

tuffet: A small stool.
curds and whey: A lumpy, soupy dish made from heating milk.
bough: A tree branch.
broth: A soup made with meat or fish.

Nursery rhymes come from many different places. Some were meant to be recited as part of a game—like a grown-up saying "Pat-a-cake, pat-a-cake" while a young child claps along. Others were originally written for adults and describe people and events from history. Many have hidden meanings that poke fun at kings or other rulers who were in power many years ago.

These poems were often written in a careful and secretive way so that no one could ever be completely sure whom the poems were about. Other nursery rhymes don't mean a thing. They're nothing more than nonsense words strung together in a way that sounds funny or pleasing to the ear.

Nursery Rhymes: Fun, usually short poems written for children and often recited at bedtime.

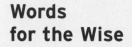

PLAY TRACK 8

"Old Mother Hubbard" was first published in 1805 in England and was a huge smash. It is said that the author, Sarah Catherine Martin, liked to talk a lot, and that she wrote the poem after someone got tired of listening to her and told her to go write a poem!

Words for the Wise

tripe: Part of an animal's stomach often served as food.

fruiterer: A fruit seller.

jig: A lively dance.

cobbler: Someone who makes and repairs shoes.

a-spinning: A way of making yarn or thread.

hosier: A seller of hose (like pantyhose, tights, or socks).

Old Mother Hubbard
by Sarah Catherine Martin

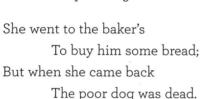

Old Mother Hubbard
Went to the cupboard,
To fetch her poor dog a bone;
But when she came there
The cupboard was bare
And so the poor dog had none.

She went to the baker's
To buy him some bread;
But when she came back
The poor dog was dead.

She went to the undertaker's
To buy him a coffin;
But when she came back
The poor dog was laughing.

She took a clean dish
To get him some **tripe**;
But when she came back
He was smoking a pipe.

She went to the alehouse,
To get him some beer;
But when she came back
The dog sat in a chair.

She went to the tavern
For white wine and red
But when she came back
The dog stood on his head.

She went to the **fruiterer's**
To buy him some fruit;
But when she came back
He was playing the flute.

She went to the tailor's
To buy him a coat;
But when she came back
He was riding a goat.

She went to the hatter's
To buy him a hat;
But when she came back
He was feeding the cat.

She went to the barber's
To buy him a wig;
But when she came back
He was dancing a **jig**.

She went to the **cobbler's**
To buy him some shoes;
But when she came back
He was reading the news.

She went to the seamstress
To buy him some linen;
But when she came back
The dog was **a-spinning**.

She went to the **hosier's**
To buy him some hose;
But when she came back
He was dressed in his clothes.

The dame made a curtsy,
The dog made a bow;
The dame said, Your servant,
The dog said, Bow-wow.

Rhymes That Prompt Laughter (If That's What You're After)
NONSENSE VERSE

While most nursery rhymes were written as entertainment for children or filled with secret meaning for adults, **nonsense verse** is just what its name says: pure nonsense.

That doesn't mean it is gibberish, however. This unusual type of poetry takes familiar things and puts them in unfamiliar settings. Poets first began writing nonsense verse in the late eighteenth century. It is said that kids often enjoy these poems more than adults, because they have better imaginations!

Nonsense verse also often features words that the writer has completely made up but that we can somehow understand, usually because a crafty poet provides

clues to what they might mean elsewhere in the poem. The wild stories and outrageous images in nonsense-verse poems usually leave readers smiling—which is what the poet is after.

This style of poetry walks the fine line between utter beauty and utter babble. And most of the time, it's funny, too. "Jabberwocky" appeared in Lewis

If You're a Poet, You Should Know It

nonsense verse: A type of poetry featuring fantastic images or made-up words that entertains through its wild silliness.

⏩ PLAY TRACK 9

Some poets spent hours, weeks—who knows, years, maybe!—finding the right word. Others couldn't be bothered and decided to just make up their own. Lewis Carroll's "Jabberwocky" is the most famous example of this technique.

You can figure out some of the strange words in "Jabberwocky" from the way they sound. (Don't you think "burbled" must be a combination of "bubbled," "babbled," and "gurgled"?) Of course, it's anyone's guess what a "Bandersnatch" is, or what exactly makes woods "tulgey." But you get the feeling Lewis Carroll wanted it that way. After all, here we are, 150 years after the poem was written, wondering what it means!

Jabberwocky

by Lewis Carroll

'Twas brillig, and the slithy toves
      Did gyre and gimble in the wabe:
All mimsy were the borogoves,
      And the mome raths outgrabe.

"Beware the Jabberwock, my son!
      The jaws that bite, the claws that catch!
Beware the Jubjub bird, and shun
      The frumious Bandersnatch!"

He took his vorpal sword in hand:
      Long time the manxome foe he sought—
So rested he by the Tumtum tree,
      And stood awhile in thought.

And, as in uffish thought he stood,
      The Jabberwock, with eyes of flame,
Came whiffling through the tulgey wood,
      And burbled as it came!

One, two! One, two! And through and through
      The vorpal blade went snicker-snack!
He left it dead, and with its head
      He went galumphing back.

"And hast thou slain the Jabberwock?
      Come to my arms, my beamish boy!
O frabjous day! Callooh! Callay!"
      He chortled in his joy.

'Twas brillig, and the slithy toves
      Did gyre and gimble in the wabe:
All mimsy were the borogoves,
      And the mome raths outgrabe.

Carroll's book *Through the Looking-Glass*, which was published in 1871 and contained the further adventures of the characters from his book *Alice in Wonderland*. In the passage to the right, Alice asks Humpty Dumpty to explain the poem "Jabberwocky" to her.

She gets as far as the first paragraph—or **stanza**, as paragraphs in a poem are called—before Humpty Dumpty cuts her off:

"That's enough to begin with," Humpty Dumpty interrupted: "there are plenty of hard words there. *'Brillig'* means four o'clock in the afternoon—the time when you begin *broiling* things for dinner."

"That'll do very well," said Alice: "and *'slithy'*?"

"Well, *'slithy'* means 'lithe and slimy.' 'Lithe' is the same as 'active.' You see it's like a **portmanteau**—there are two meanings packed up into one word."

"I see it now," Alice remarked thoughtfully: "and what are *'toves'*?"

"Well, *'toves'* are something like badgers—they're something like Lizards—and they're something like corkscrews."

"They must be very curious-looking creatures."

"They are that," said Humpty Dumpty, "also they make their nests under sun-dials—also they live on cheese."

"And what's to *'gyre'* and to *'gimble'*?"

"To *'gyre'* is to go round and round like a gyroscope. To *'gimble'* is to make holes like a **gimlet**."

"And *'the wabe'* is the grass-plot round a sun-dial, I suppose?" said Alice, surprised at her own ingenuity.

"Of course it is. It's called *'wabe'* you know, because it goes a long way before it, and a long way behind it—"

"And a long way beyond it on each side," Alice added.

"Exactly so. Well then, *'mimsy'* is 'flimsy and miserable' (there's another portmanteau for you). And a *'borogove'* is a thin shabby-looking bird with its feathers sticking out all round—something like a live mop."

"And then *'mome raths'*?" said Alice. "I'm afraid I'm giving you a great deal of trouble."

"Well, a *'rath'* is a sort of green pig: but *'mome'* I'm not certain about. I think it's short for 'from home'—meaning that they'd lost their way, you know."

"And what does *'outgrabe'* mean?"

"Well *'outgribing'* is something between bellowing and whistling, with a kind of sneeze in the middle: however, you'll hear it done, maybe—down in the wood yonder—and, when you've once heard it, you'll be *quite* content. . . ."

Nineteen Lines but Just Two Rhymes
THE VILLANELLE

Poets who write nonsense verse seem to have a lot of freedom when it comes to writing poems. Afterall, they can make up their own words! But for the poor author of the **villanelle**, there are a lot of tricky rules to follow.

The villanelle has two main lines that are repeated again and again throughout the poem like the chorus of a song. Those lines are what make the villanelle one of the most powerful forms of poetry, and poets craft them very carefully. As these lines are repeated, the feelings they express—happiness, sadness, anger—get stronger every time.

VILLANELLE is pronounced like "villain" (as in bad guy) and the letter "l." (The last "e" is silent.)

THE STRUCTURE OF A POEM
(An Arboreal Analogy)

Triplet = 3 lines
STANZA

Quatrain = 4 lines
STANZA

The **structure** of a villanelle, or the way the lines and rhymes are arranged, is very specific. It's made up of six stanzas. Five of the stanzas are called **triplets** because they have three lines. One stanza is different from all the others and therefore stands out. It is a **quatrain**, or a stanza of four lines. Take a look at the poem on page 19 as an example. The two memorable lines are introduced in the opening stanza. Then they repeat at the end of the next four stanzas. The final stanza ends by repeating the two memorable lines once again.

Villanelles were first used by French and Italian poets. In the nineteenth and twentieth centuries, poets writing in English started using the style.

Some people say that Dylan Thomas's poem **"Do Not Go Gentle into That Good Night,"** published in 1951, is the best villanelle ever written. Like many poets, Thomas often wrote about love and death. His poems are powerful but often sad. He wrote this poem for his father at a time when his father was old, sick, and nearing death.

When you read the poem, however, you will notice that the words do not always directly refer to his father or to death. Instead, Thomas uses symbols to express what he means. "Why doesn't he just come out and say it?" you might ask. Well, by using symbols, Thomas stirs different thoughts in our heads. We make emotional connections between the symbol and the actual meaning—feelings that are sometimes stronger than if you'd just said something straight out. In this poem, you can almost picture Dylan Thomas kneeling at his father's bedside, begging him to be strong.

⚷ PLAY TRACK 10

You might think that a poem would get tiring if the poet kept repeating the same lines over and over. But Dylan Thomas was a true master. In this poem, he didn't change the two main lines: "Do not go gentle into that good night" and "Rage, rage against the dying of the light." Instead, he changed the way we read them. In the first stanza, the lines are orders to his father to keep fighting against death. But in the next four stanzas, the lines describe what other men—wise men, good men, wild men, grave (or serious) men—face when confronting death. The words are the same, but the meaning changes.

The Villanelle Uses Only Two Rhymes

1: The first and third lines of each stanza rhyme with each other—and they rhyme with the first and third lines of every other stanza.

For example, in Dylan Thomas's "Do Not Go Gentle into That Good Night" the words "night" and "light" in the first stanza rhyme, and they rhyme with the words "right" and "night" in the second stanza, and so forth through the poem.

2: The second line of each stanza rhymes with the second line of every other stanza.

In Thomas's poem "day" rhymes with "they," which rhymes with "bay" and so on.

If You're a Poet, You Should Know It

villanelle: A nineteen-line poem with carefully arranged rhymes.

structure: The way a poem is organized. Usually this means how long the poem is, how many lines are in each stanza, and whether or not words rhyme.

triplet: A stanza made up of three lines (just like a *triple* in baseball is when a batter makes it to three bases).

quatrain: A stanza made up of four lines (just like four *quarters* make up a dollar).

symbol: An image selected by a writer to represent something else, like "light" meaning "life," or "dark" meaning "death." The use of symbols in a poem or story is called **symbolism**.

Do Not Go Gentle into That Good Night *

by Dylan Thomas

Do not go gentle into that good night,
Old age should burn and rave at close of day;
Rage, rage against the dying of the light.

Though wise men at their end know dark is right,
Because their words had forked no lightning they
Do not go gentle into that good night.

Good men, the last wave by, crying how bright
Their frail deeds might have danced in a green bay,
Rage, rage against the dying of the light.

Wild men who caught and sang the sun in flight,
And learn, too late, they grieved it on its way,
Do not go gentle into that good night.

Grave men, near death, who see with blinding sight
Blind eyes could blaze like meteors and be gay,
Rage, rage against the dying of the light.

And you, my father, there on the sad height,
Curse, bless, me now with your fierce tears, I pray.
Do not go gentle into that good night.
Rage, rage against the dying of the light.

In the first stanza of this poem, Dylan Thomas is urging his father to fight against death, which he describes as the "dying of the light." In the next four stanzas, Thomas describes how others have struggled:

Brilliant men who never wrote a bestseller, never gave a speech that sparked a revolution

People who helped others but, by chance, received little credit

Those who spent their lives dancing and playing, and realized later that life is not just for games

Men who lived strict, careful lives, only to discover, too late, the fun they missed

As he ends the poem, Thomas again tells his father to fight. It's like an army general telling his soldiers to never give up, no matter how bad things look. The last mark you make on the world should be a great one.

There Once Was a Poem So Outrageous, Read Aloud, It Became Quite Contagious
THE LIMERICK

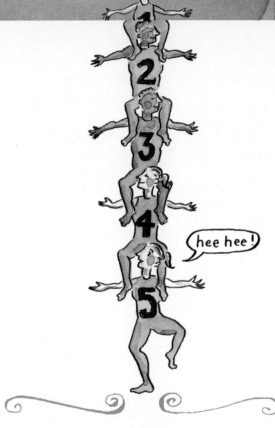

hee hee!

F ew styles of poetry are as easy to follow or as fun to recite as the limerick. There's seldom anything tricky about these. They're short—only five lines—silly, and simple, which seems to be why folks love them so much. Limericks are thought to have been around for about two hundred years, but the first collection of them wasn't published until 1846 by the poet Edward Lear.

No one knows for sure how the limerick got its name. Limerick is a county in Ireland, but its connection to the poem isn't exactly clear. Some say the poem's name is based on a verse that crowds used to sing at nineteenth-century parties to encourage poets to read one of their poems: "Will you come up to Limerick?" Others say it was named after a group of poets in Limerick who liked the form. However it got its name, people didn't begin referring to the short, five-line poems as "limericks" until around 1900. Then the name stuck.

Limerick writers have made a habit of finding the humor in accidents and other unpleasant situations (not unlike how we giggle at Wile E. Coyote's mishaps when he's chasing the Road Runner around in cartoons). It's hard not to laugh at some of the situations described in the limericks on the next page.

5 LINES are ALL YOU NEED!

The limerick has a structure that's easy to follow. The first and second lines rhyme. The third and fourth lines are shorter and rhyme with each other. Then the final line rhymes with the first two lines. This last line is usually where the humor comes in—it often contains an unexpected turn of events, or a surprise that makes readers suddenly look at the rest of the poem in a different way (usually with a smile).

Limerick: **A short, humorous, five-line poem.**

PLAY TRACK 13

A flea and a fly in a **flue**
Were imprisoned, so what could they do?
Said the fly, "Let us flee,"
"Let us fly," said the flea.
So they flew through a flaw in the flue.

...tt Burgess

There was a young lady named Hannah,
Who slipped on a peel of banana.
More stars she **espied**
As she lay on her side
Than are found in the Star Spangled Banner.

A gentleman sprang to assist her;
He picked up her glove and her **wrister**;
"Did you fall, Ma'am?" he cried;
"Do you think," she replied,
"I sat down for the fun of it, Mister?"

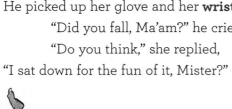

PLAY TRACK 14

A sleeper from the Amazon
Put nighties of his gra'mazon
The reason, that
He was too fat
To get his own pajamazon.

PLAY TRACK 15

There once was a man from Nantucket,
Who kept all his cash in a bucket,
But his daughter named Nan
Ran away with a man,
And alas for the bucket, Nan-tuck-et!

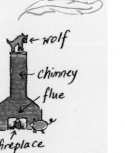
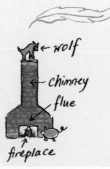

But he followed the pair to Pawtucket,
The man and the girl with the bucket,
And he said to the man,
He was welcome to Nan;
And as for the bucket, Paw-tuck-et!

Words for the Wise

espied: The act of having seen (or spied) something.

wrister: A knitted scarf for the hands and wrists.

flue: A passageway connecting a fireplace and a chimney.

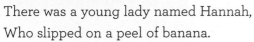

← wolf
← chimney
flue
fireplace

Poets often use clever wordplay in limericks to change the meaning of words, or to say two things at once. In the two limericks above, for example, **Nantucket** and **Pawtucket** end up referring to more than just places in New England.

The First Limerick

Many limericks have traditionally started with the words "There was"—an opening that works in describing just about anything. Edward Lear, the father of the limerick, said he particularly liked the line "There was an old man of Tobago," because he was able to think of so many rhymes to use with it.

There was an old man of **Tobago**,
Who lived on rice, gruel, and **sago**;
Till, much to his **bliss**,
    His physician said this—
To a leg, sir, of **mutton** you may go.

Words for the Wise

Tobago: An island in South America.
sago: A pasty, untasty pudding.
bliss: Ultimate happiness.
mutton: Lamb's meat.

No one knows the authors of many of the most famous limericks. Instead, these poems are referred to as having been written by Anonymous—someone whose identity remains a mystery.

Many authors—not just of limericks—have chosen to remain anonymous. There are a number of reasons why a writer may choose to do so. Even a hundred years ago, women writers were not taken as seriously as men, so some women wrote under a man's name—or under no name at all. Other writers thought their poems might get them into trouble, for example, if they questioned the king or other rulers, so they left their names off their work.

◆ PLAY TRACK 16

Many consider this strange old poem the original limerick, and it was the one that inspired Edward Lear to collect limericks in his *Book of Nonsense*, which was published in 1846. The poem describes a man under a doctor's orders to eat healthy foods, including sago (pronounced "say-go"), which was not a particularly tasty paste. The man is very pleased ("much to his bliss") when the doctor allows him to have a leg of mutton (or as we might call it, lamb chops).

Others didn't think anyone would be interested in their poems, so they never bothered putting their names on them in the first place! Limericks were fun poems, but they were considered rather rude and crude in their day and not taken very seriously. We still laugh at them today, and at the same time we wonder who the clever authors might have been.

If You're a Poet, You Should Know It

anonymous: The term used for the author of a poem when the original writer is unknown.

Go away! Don't look at what I'm writing!

There was a young lady from Niger,
Who smiled as she rode on a tiger;
    They returned from the ride
    With the lady inside,
And the smile on the face of the tiger.

"Nonsense pure and absolute."
—Edward Lear, describing his poems

There was a young man from the city,
Who met what he thought was a kitty;
    He gave it a pat,
    And said, "Nice little cat!"
And they buried his clothes out of pity.

There was a young girl named O'Neill
Who went up in the great Ferris Wheel;
    But when half way around
    She looked at the ground,
It cost her an eighty-cent meal.

There was an Old Man with a beard,
Who said, "It is just as I feared! –
    Two owls and a hen,
    Four larks and a wren,
Have all built their nests in my beard."
          —Edward Lear

There was an old man of Madrid
Who was hit with a brick by a kid;
    Said the man, "Oh, what joy
    To wallup that boy!
Be darned if I don't;" and he did.
          —Gelett Burgess

Haikus Have Three Lines and
Seventeen Syllables Simple, Beautiful
THE HAIKU

Hundreds of years ago, Japanese poets invented the **haiku,** a form of poetry very different from styles used by English writers.

The first thing you'll notice about the haiku is how small it is. The traditional haiku has only three lines. And those lines are short. All together, the poem is only seventeen **syllables** (or beats) long.

Lines and syllables are one thing, but what *really* makes the haiku special is what it's about. Traditional haikus describe a single image—like a butterfly landing on a flower, or a raindrop splashing in a puddle—that makes us think about nature. And the images described in haikus are meant to bring to mind a certain season and remind us of the special feelings that accompany that time of year. Modern poets have expanded the subjects of haikus to include just about anything—not just nature and the changing seasons—but the strictest of haiku writers still say the poems should follow the old rules.

Haikus were made famous by three Japanese poets born in the sixteenth and seventeenth centuries. Matsuo Bashō, Yosa Buson, and Kobayashi Issa each wrote in their native Japanese about nature and the seasons—the traditional subject of the haiku—and their words are still read and translated into new languages today.

Haikus are usually written with careful attention to how their seventeen syllables are arranged. The most popular form has five syllables in the first line, seven syllables in the second line, and five syllables in the third line. See if you can count the lines and the syllables in this example:

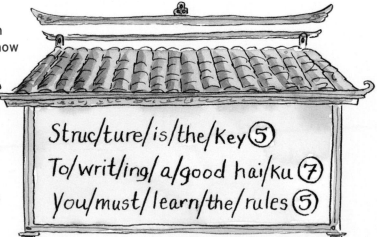

Struc/ture/is/the/key ⑤
To/writ/ing/a/good hai/ku ⑦
You/must/learn/the/rules ⑤

➡ PLAY TRACK 22

Haikus rarely tell stories. Instead, they paint the picture and leave the story up to us. Who's to say which is the "proper" way to interpret a haiku? Maybe the poet wanted readers to think about winter. Or about bugs. Or just about being happy, or sad. That's what's most fun about the haiku—it's up to us.

A HAIKU FOR EVERY SEASON

Popsicle melting.
Red stains on sticky fingers
Wash off in the pool.

The snowball lands—thump!
White flecks upon the window
Eyes peek out—who's there?

Slender, silver trout
Wiggling in the shallow stream
Spots a worm—my worm.

The tree's a pumpkin:
Round, and brilliant orange. Look quick!
Soon, a skeleton.

If You're a Poet, You Should Know It

haiku: A short poem of three lines and seventeen syllables describing nature and often a particular time of year.

syllable: Individual parts of a word, like beats in a musical measure. "Cat" has one beat, or one syllable. "Basket" has two syllables: bas-ket. "Superman" has three syllables: su-per-man.

Gather Round for a Story of Heroes and Glory
NARRATIVE VERSE

In the early days, writers of poems weren't writers at all. Most of them didn't even know how to write! Instead, poems were read aloud, or sometimes sung.

Types of narrative verse: Narrative verse comes in many shapes and sizes. **Epics** are long stories with many parts. Some are as long as a whole book! **Romances** are usually shorter and glorify heroic deeds, like a knight saving a princess from a horrible dragon.
Historical verse takes true stories and relates them in the form of a poem (though sometimes stretching the truth).

Those early poems were called **narrative verse** and were composed as a way of telling stories. Writers (though they might as well be called "rememberers," since they never wrote anything down) told elaborate tales to entertain people, and as a way of recording the history of their people. These were the first poems. Nearly three thousand years ago, Greek poets swapped stories this way and some of those tales are still told today.

There are many forms of narrative verse. One form is **historical verse**, which retold true events in the form of a poem. Skilled poets could make history **exciting**! They took true stories and described them with a rhyme and a rhythm that brought those tales to life.

"**Paul Revere's Ride**" is a famous example of historical verse, capturing one of the most celebrated moments in American history.

If You're a Poet, You Should Know It

narrative verse: A story told in the form of a poem. The word "narrative" comes from **narrator**—one who tells stories. **Verse** is another word for poetry.

◆◆ PLAY TRACK 23

(Select passages are printed here. You can listen to a longer version of the poem on the website. If you are following along with the website, stars indicate the gaps.)

"Paul Revere's Ride" describes a dangerous and exciting event that took place at the beginning of the American Revolution. On the night of April 18, 1775, British soldiers began marching into Boston, Massachusetts to seize weapons that the American colonists had collected. When the nightwatchman, Paul Revere, saw them, he made his famous late-night ride on horseback to warn the colonists that the British were coming. Listen to the quick pace of the words and the short, choppy phrases. You can't help but read it fast, and you can almost hear the horse's hooves clip-clopping on the New England cobblestones!

Paul Revere's Ride

by Henry Wadsworth Longfellow

Listen, my children, and you shall hear
Of the midnight ride of Paul Revere,
On the eighteenth of April, in Seventy-Five;
Hardly a man is now alive
Who remembers that famous day and year.

He said to his friend, "If the British march
By land or sea from the town to-night,
Hang a lantern aloft in the **belfry** arch
Of the North Church tower as a signal light,—
One, if by land, and two, if by sea;
And I on the opposite shore will be,
Ready to ride and spread the alarm
Through every Middlesex village and farm,
For the country folk to be up and to arm."

☆ ★ ☆ ☆ ★ ☆ ★ ☆

A hurry of hoofs in a village street,
A shape in the moonlight, a bulk in the dark,
And beneath, from the pebbles, in passing, a spark
Struck out by a steed flying fearless and fleet;

That was all! And yet, through the gloom and the light,
The fate of a nation was riding that night;
And the spark struck out by that steed, in his flight,
Kindled the land into flame with its heat.

☆ ★ ☆ ☆ ★ ☆ ★ ☆

So through the night rode Paul Revere;
And so through the night went his cry of alarm
To every Middlesex village and farm,—
A cry of **defiance** and not of fear,
A voice in the darkness, a knock at the door,
And a word that shall echo forevermore!
For, **borne** on the night-wind of the Past,
Through all our history, to the last,
In the hour of darkness and peril and need,
The people will waken and listen to hear
The hurrying hoof-beats of that **steed**,
And the midnight message of Paul Revere.

Words for the Wise

belfry: A church bell tower.
defiance: A courageous fight against authority.
borne: Carried along.
steed: A horse (especially a fast and high-spirited one!)

April 18, 1775

My Dear, Aren't You Smitten by These Words That I've Written?
LYRIC VERSE

Some poets wrote as a way of telling stories, but other poets wanted to express feelings, like love, sadness, joy, and grief. To do so, these writers turned to **lyric verse**.

Lyric verse is different from narrative poetry in many ways. While narrative poetry tells fantastic tales, lyric poetry is written to stir emotions within you. While narrative poetry can be long and rambling, lyric poetry, on the other hand, is usually shorter and easier to follow. Lyric poets often make steady use of rhyming words and carefully arrange the lines within each stanza. (The villanelle we learned about earlier is just one example of the many types of lyric verse.)

You can think of a narrative poem as a comic book—lots of action and excitement. Lyric poetry is more like that great song you keep hearing on the radio, the one that sticks in your head and that, for reasons you're not quite sure of, makes you sad, or thoughtful or happy. Robert Burns's lyric poem **"A Red, Red Rose"** is about what seems to be many poets' favorite topic: love.

STUCK IN ELEGY MODE

ODE TO A COMMODE

Like narrative verse, lyric verse has been around since the days of the Greeks. It can take many forms. An **elegy** is a sad poem, usually written in memory of someone who has died. **Odes** tend to be longer and honor a specific person or thing. (One of the most famous odes is John Keats's "Ode on a Grecian Urn." It's fifty lines long and is about a vase!) **Sonnets** and **pastorals** are other forms of lyric verse, but we'll learn more about them later.

◀▶ PLAY TRACK 24

Robert Burns was a hopeless romantic who was always falling in love with someone or other, then writing a poem about her. He grew up on a farm in the Scottish countryside during the eighteenth century, and many of the words he uses were not proper English of his day, but instead were slang words (kind of like when we say "cool" and "gotcha" today). Burns often wrote words the way they were pronounced. But even when they are spelled differently, it's usually pretty easy to understand the meaning, and the special language helps us to hear the poem the way Burns himself might have read it back in 1796, the year the poem was first published.

To show how dedicated he is to his beloved, Robert Burns compares his feelings to other items of beauty, like a rose or a pretty melody. In the third stanza, he says his "luve" will last forever—until the sun melts and the seas run dry. And in the last stanza, he says he'd travel ten thousand miles to be with his love. That's like walking the distance between New York City and Los Angeles—four times!

A Red, Red Rose

by Robert Burns

I.

O, my luve is like a red, red rose,
    That's newly sprung in June,
O, my luve is like the melodie,
    That's sweetly play'd in tune.

II.

As fair art thou, my **bonie** lass,
    So deep in luve am I
And I will luve thee still, my dear
    Till a' the seas gang dry.

III.

Till a' the seas gang dry, my dear,
    And the rocks melt wi' the sun!
And I will luve thee still, my dear,
    While the sands o' life shall run.

IV.

And **fare** thee weel, my only luve,
    And fare thee weel a while!
And I will come again, my luve,
    Tho' it were ten thousand mile!

Words for the Wise

romantic: Someone who is passionate, easily love-struck, sensitive, and thoughtful.
bonie: Pretty or attractive.
fare: To experience something (to "fare well" is to do well).

A Poem Fantastic (Though Usually Old)
That May Teach a Lesson (so It's Often Retold)
THE BALLAD

The **ballad** is a form of narrative verse that was especially popular during the Middle Ages and was later used by many English poets. It's different than the narrative poems we learned about earlier in several ways. For one thing, ballads are usually on the shorter side, although they can still be pretty long compared to some other poetic styles. And the action within ballads tends to rise to an exciting **climax**.

Ballad writers often chose a story with **supernatural** elements, like ghosts or demons or other spooky characters. There's often a lesson to be learned in a ballad, too—but these aren't lessons like "finish your vegetables" or "clean your room." Instead, they're lessons about fairness and justice and doing what's right. The stories behind most ballads are sad

ones, as the poet recounts a miserable tragedy, like a loved one who disappeared, breaking the poet's heart.

One great example of a ballad is Robert Browning's **"The Pied Piper of Hamelin."** This particular ballad isn't about lost love but about lost children. The event it describes supposedly took place in Germany in the year 1284. Since then, the tale has been retold many times by many people, but never with as much magic and sparkle as in Browning's 1842 poem.

The expression "pay the piper" comes from the story of the Pied Piper, and it has come to represent suffering the consequences of an earlier action.

◗◆ PLAY TRACK 25

Robert Browning was a nineteenth-century British writer of poems and plays. "The Pied Piper of Hamelin" is one of his most famous works and was written for the young son of one of Browning's friends. Browning's fun rhymes and vivid images paint colorful pictures in the readers' heads. Have a listen to some of the poem. The narrator will fill you in on the parts that are missing. You can find and read the entire poem at the library or the bookstore.

Fairness & Justice

The Pied Piper of Hamelin

by Robert Browning

In Germany hundreds of years ago, the residents of a small village called Hamelin were hopelessly plagued by one particular furry nuisance—or so the legend goes . . .

Rats!
They fought the dogs and killed the cats,
 And bit the babies in the cradles,
And ate the cheeses out of the vats,
 And licked the soup from the cook's own ladles,
Split open the kegs of salted **sprats**,
Made nests inside men's Sunday hats,
And even spoiled the women's chats,
 By drowning their speaking
 With shrieking and squeaking
In fifty different sharps and flats. . . .

The village leaders were desperate to rid the town of the rats. While meeting at town hall to develop a plan, a stranger suddenly appeared.

His queer long coat from heel to head
Was half of yellow and half of red,
And he himself was tall and thin,
With sharp blue eyes, each like a pin,
And light loose hair, yet swarthy skin,
No **tuft** on cheek nor beard on chin,
But lips where smiles went out and in;
There was no guessing his **kith** and **kin**. . . .

Because of his strange, multicolored clothing, the fellow called himself the Pied Piper ("pied" being an old-fashioned way of describing something with many colors). The Piper promised the townspeople that he would lead all the rats out of the village—for a tidy fee. The mayor quickly agreed, and the Pied Piper raised his flute to his lips.

And ere three shrill notes the pipe uttered,
You heard as if an army muttered;
And the muttering grew to a grumbling;
And the grumbling grew to a mighty rumbling;
And out of the houses the rats came tumbling.
Great rats, small rats, lean rats, **brawny** rats,
Brown rats, black rats, gray rats, **tawny** rats,
Grave old plodders, gay young friskers,
 Fathers, mothers, uncles, cousins,
Cocking tails and pricking whiskers,
 Families by tens and dozens,
Brothers, sisters, husbands, wives—
Followed the piper for their lives.
From street to street he piped advancing,
And step by step they followed dancing, . . .

With the rats gone, the villagers rejoiced. But when the Pied Piper asked for his payment, the mayor went back on his word and offered him only a tiny sum. So the Piper picked up his flute once again and began to blow.

Pied Piper (continued)

There was a rustling that seemed like a bustling
Of merry crowds **justling** at pitching and hustling;
Small feet were pattering, wooden shoes clattering,
Little hands clapping and little tongues chattering,
And, like **fowls** in a farm-yard when barley is scattering,
Out came the children running.
All the little boys and girls,
With rosy cheeks and **flaxen** curls,
And sparkling eyes and teeth like pearls,
Tripping and skipping, ran merrily after
The wonderful music with shouting and laughter. . . .
When, lo, as they reached the mountain-side,
A wondrous portal opened wide,
As if a cavern was suddenly hollowed;
And the Piper advanced and the children followed,
And when all were in to the very last,
The door in the mountain-side shut fast. . . .

With that, the children disappeared, never to be seen again, and the people of Hamelin learned a harsh lesson about keeping a promise.

Broadside ballads were poems printed on large sheets of paper that looked like newspaper pages. These poems offered colorful, sometimes exaggerated (what we today would call "sensationalized") retellings of current news events. They were popular from the sixteenth century all the way up to the twentieth century.

Words for the Wise

pied: Containing many colors in patterns and patches.

sprats: A type of fish that could be preserved with salt and eaten later.

tuft: A patch of hair.

kith and kin: Friends, neighbors, and family.

ere: Before.

brawny: Strong and muscular.

tawny: Blond or brownish.

justling: Jiggling or shaking, like jostling.

fowl: Barnyard birds (like chickens).

flaxen: Pale yellow or blond.

Sheep, Shepherds, and Other Sappy Stuff
THE PASTORAL

Alas, when some people think of poetry, they think of long-winded writers going on and on about the beauty of the sun shining on cows munching hay in a quiet pasture—and boring us all to tears in the process.

Those folks probably read one too many **pastoral** poems. This particular form of poetry offers a romanticized, **idealistic** image of how great things are in the country, or in the woods, or on a farm. The things pastoral poems describe—sheep, flowers, and honey, for example—are sweet and happy and fun to think about, though they're not particularly realistic.

But that's the point. Pastoral poems are a way of escaping to another world far from the misery and corruption that was sometimes associated with city life—a faraway world where everything's perfect and troubles don't exist.

And the great pastoral poets sure could paint a pretty picture of the simple life. It's enough to make the most sophisticated city dweller want to move to the country!

Like many forms of verse, pastoral poems about simple country living were first written by the Greeks. Italians later copied the style. In the sixteenth century, English poets began writing pastorals, like the two examples on the following pages.

If You're a Poet, You Should Know It

pastoral: A lyric verse about shepherds, nature, or country living.
idealistic: Fanciful or not very grounded in real life.

"Poetry is the record of the best and happiest moments of the happiest and best minds."

—*Percy Bysshe Shelley, nineteenth-century poet*

The Passionate Shepherd to His Love

Christopher Marlowe's "The Passionate Shepherd to His Love" was written in the late sixteenth century and is a classic example of the pastoral poem. In it, the shepherd makes an earnest plea to his beloved to come away with him to enjoy the simple life in the country. He promises a wonderful world filled with birds singing beautiful lullabies and an endless supply of pretty flowers. (It's a little corny, sure—but winning the heart of a fair damsel was different back before movie theaters and fancy restaurants.)

Words for the Wise

madrigal: A love song from medieval times.
posies, myrtle: Wildflowers.
kirtle: A woman's dress.
swain: Someone who lives in the country.

by Christopher Marlowe

Come live with me and be my love,
And we will all the pleasures prove
That valleys, groves, hills, and fields,
Woods, or steepy mountain yields.

And we will sit upon the rocks,
Seeing the shepherds feed their flocks,
By shallow rivers to whose falls
Melodious birds sing **madrigals**.

And I will make thee beds of roses,
And a thousand fragrant **posies**,
A cap of flowers, and a **kirtle**,
Embroidered all with leaves of **myrtle**;

A gown made of the finest wool
Which from our pretty lambs we pull;
Fair lined slippers for the cold,
With buckles of the purest gold;

A belt of straw and ivy buds,
With coral clasps and amber studs:
And if these pleasures may thee move,
Come live with me and be my love.

The shepherds' **swains** shall dance and sing
For thy delight each May morning.
If these delights thy mind may move,
Then live with me and be my love.

The Nymph's Reply to the Shepherd

by Sir Walter Raleigh

If all the world and love were young,
And truth in every shepherd's tongue,
These pretty pleasures might me move
To live with thee and be thy love.

Time drives the flocks from field to fold,
When rivers rage and rocks grow cold,
And **Philomel** becometh dumb;
The rest complains of cares to come.

The flowers do fade, and **wanton fields**
To wayward winter reckoning yields;
A honey tongue, a heart of **gall**,
Is fancy's spring, but sorrow's fall.

Thy gowns, thy shoes, thy beds of roses,
Thy cap, thy kirtle, and thy posies
Soon break, soon **wither**, soon forgotten—
In folly ripe, in reason rotten.

The belt of straw and ivy buds,
Thy coral clasps and amber studs,
All these in me no means can move
To come to thee and be thy love.

But could youth last and love still breed,
Had joys no date nor age no need,
Then these delights my mind might move
To live with thee and be thy love.

Words for the Wise

nymph: A beautiful maiden, often possessing mystical powers, who lives in the woods or the mountains.

Philomel: Princess who, according to Greek legend, was turned into a nightingale.

wanton fields: Fields that are not well attended.

gall: Bitter juices produced by your internal organs.

wither: To shrivel up.

Poems of Feelings and Hearts Shining Bright (They're a Pleasure to Hear, but a Devil to Write)
THE SONNET

English poets began writing sonnets in the sixteenth century, copying a style that Italian poets had invented two hundred years earlier. The sonnet followed careful rules about length and **rhyme scheme.**

Sonnets were a popular way for poets to express their feelings (especially love!), and famous writers, like William Shakespeare, favored them. They weren't written much after the sixteenth century, though a few famous poets would try a sonnet now and then. The rules are so particular that these poems are just plain tough to write. But at its best, the sonnet builds slowly to an outpouring of

feeling, making it an especially expressive type of poem.

Hundreds of years ago, people who spoke English sometimes used words that sound funny to us today. But that's how they really spoke, and if you read carefully, you can usually figure out what they meant. "Thee," "thou," and "thy" were other ways of saying "you" and "yours." Sometimes, writers would replace the "s" at the end of a word with "th" or "'st." (Isn't it more fun to say "hath" and "wand'rest" than plain old "has" and "wanders"?)

William "14 LINES OR BUST" Shakespeare

Sonnets are usually made up of fourteen lines, but beyond that, there are many different variations (each one more complicated than the last!). The form we're most familiar with is the **Shakespearean sonnet**, used by—who else?—William Shakespeare. In a Shakespearean sonnet, the fourteen lines are divided into four parts: three quatrains and a **couplet** (or a two-line stanza). The first and third lines of the quatrains rhyme, as do the second and fourth lines. Both lines in the couplet rhyme with each other. And those last two lines are special in another way—they're often the climax where the emotion really pours out. Sounds tricky, I know—but take a look at the sonnet on the next page and you'll see what I mean.

Yes, I stole thy money out of thy wallet...

If You're a Poet, You Should Know It

rhyme scheme: The way the words that rhyme are arranged within a poem.

Shakespearean sonnet: A fourteen-line poem made up of three quatrains and a couplet.

couplet: A stanza made up of two lines (just like two people are called a couple).

Sonnet 18

by William Shakespeare

Shall I compare thee to a summer's day?
Thou art more lovely and more temperate:
Rough winds do shake the darling buds of May,
And summer's lease hath all too short a date:
Sometimes too hot the eye of heaven shines,
And often is his gold complexion dimmed;
And every fair from fair sometime declines,
By chance or nature's changing course untrimmed;
But thy eternal summer shall not fade,
Nor lose possession of that fair thou ow'st;
Nor shall death brag thou wander'st in his shade,
When in eternal lines to time thou grow'st:
So long as men can breathe, or eyes can see,
So long lives this, and this gives life to thee.

He's talking about me, me, ME! Be-YOO-tiful ME!

◀▶ PLAY TRACK 28

In Sonnet 18, published in 1609, William Shakespeare describes the lovely woman who has stolen his heart. The first quatrain says her beauty outlasts the beauty of summer—which, after all, ends in autumn. And his beloved is gentle—unlike summer, whose "rough winds" can damage the "darling buds" of the flowers in May.

The next quatrain points out that the sun—"the eye of heaven"—can shine too warm, or can be dimmed by clouds. And the summertime has to lose its luster eventually—"every fair [or something great] from fair sometimes declines." But, as Shakespeare writes in the third quatrain and the final couplet, his lover's beauty—her "eternal summer"—lasts forever, "so long as men can breathe or eyes can see."

Words for the Wise

temperate: Warm and comfortable, usually describing weather.
complexion: The skin on someone's face.

The word "sonnet" comes from the Italian word *sonnetto*, which means "little sound."

When You Haven't Got Time to Think of a Rhyme
FREE VERSE

Not all writers care to follow strict rules about how poems should be written—like how many lines they should be, or which words must rhyme.

In the twentieth century, poets turned to **free verse** as a form without any rules. Just like the name said, these writers were free to craft their verses any way they wanted. The poems could be long or short, with lots of rhyming, some rhyming, or no rhyming at all.

Although there are no rules, that doesn't mean free verse is easy to write. Poets spend just as much time perfecting a poem in this style as they would in any other.

Though free verse became a leading form of poetry in the twentieth century, many famous poets from years ago used the same independent style, such as Walt Whitman, William Blake, and John Milton. They just didn't have a name for it yet!

E. E. Cummings, who wrote during the first half of the twentieth century, was a famous master of free verse. His wild style of poetry was often as fun to look at as to read. He seldom used punctuation, and when he did, he used it in unusual ways that didn't quite follow what we're taught in school. He almost never used capital letters—even in his own name—and as in **"Hist Whist,"** his words often danced on the page.

Free verse is the English version of the French form *vers libre* (pronounced "vares lebruh"), which was popular with French poets in the late nineteenth century.

If You're a Poet, You Should Know It

free verse: A style of poetry with no set length or rhyme scheme; its only rule is that it has no rules.

◖◗ PLAY TRACK 29

In "Hist Whist" E. E. Cummings stacks short words in brief lines, and you can't help but read them quickly. The poem is broken up so that the words almost skitter across the page—just like the ghosts, devils, and other mysterious spooks he describes.

Hist Whist

by E.E. Cummings

hist   whist
little ghostthings
tip-toe
twinkle-toe

little twitchy   ach   the great
witches and tingling
goblins   green
hob-a-nob   hob-a-nob   dancing
                                                  devil
little hoppy happy   devil
toad in tweeds
tweeds   devil
little itchy mousies   devil

with scuttling   wheeEEE
eyes   rustle and run and
hidehidehide
whisk

whisk   look out for the old woman
with the wart on her nose
what she'll do to yer
nobody knows
for she knows the devil   ooch
the devil   ouch
the devil

Alphabet Poems, Riddles, Epitaphs, and Other Unusual Styles
POEMS PECULIAR

In addition to the many well-known styles of poetry, like sonnets, haikus, and limericks, there are lots of other forms that poets have developed over the years. Each has a special way of helping writers express themselves.

Here's an assortment of some of these lesser- known but no less fun styles of poetry.

Alphabet Poems: As you'd probably suspect, an alphabet poem is written so that the reader slowly works his or her way through the alphabet, all the way from A to Z. The one on the following page was a nursery rhyme—you can imagine a father reading it to his son or daughter as a quick lesson at bedtime. Versions of this poem have been told for more than three hundred years.

Shaped Poetry: Writers using this form arrange their lines on the page so that the shape tells something about the poem.

In the seventeenth century, few people could read and write, so the shape of the poem helped to give meaning to the words. Those who could read and write were often priests or other members of the church. Because of that, many of the poems we have from those days are religious poems. George Herbert's "Easter Wings" is a good example of this kind of poem.

Riddle Poems: For centuries, writers have wrapped riddles inside poems to puzzle us. You probably know the most famous riddle poem by heart, "Humpty Dumpty." Can you figure out answers to the rest of the riddle poems on the next page?

Epitaphs: An inscription carved into a tombstone is called an epitaph. Epitaphs usually say something about the deceased's life or the circumstances of his or her death, or they have a message from beyond the grave intended for anyone who reads the inscription. Sometimes they're funny, and sometimes they're a little creepy!

There are many famous epitaphs that have been written as poems. However, in many cases, it's hard to say which ones really appear on tombstones somewhere and which were just made up to entertain us.

THE POETRY MUSE MEETS THE PECULIAR MUSE

🔊 PLAY TRACK 30

Alphabet Poem

A was an apple-pie;
B bit it,
C cut it,
D dealt it,
E eats it,
F fought for it,
G got it,
H had it,
I inspected it,
J jumped for it,
K kept it,
L longed for it,
M mourned for it,
N nodded at it,
O opened it,
P peeped in it,
Q quartered it,
R ran for it,
S stole it,
T took it,
U upset it,
V viewed it,
W wanted it,
X, Y, Z and **ampersand**
All wished for a piece in hand.

🔊 PLAY TRACK 31

Easter Wings

Lord, who createdst man in wealth and **store**,
Though foolishly he lost the same,
Decaying more and more
Till he became
Most poor:
With thee
O let me rise
As **larks**, harmoniously,
And sing this day thy victories:
Then shall the fall further the flight in me.

My tender age in sorrow did begin;
And still with sicknesses and shame
Thou didst so punish sin,
That I became
Most thin.
With thee
Let me combine,
And feel this day thy victory;
For, if I **imp** my wing on thine,
Affliction shall advance the flight in me.
—George Herbert

Riddle Poems

🔊 PLAY TRACK 32

Humpty Dumpty sat on a wall,
Humpty Dumpty had a great fall.
All the king's horses
And all the king's men
Couldn't put Humpty together again.

🔊 PLAY TRACK 33

Black I am and much admired,
Men may seek me till they're tired,
When they find me they break my head,
And take me from my resting bed.

Words for the Wise

ampersand: The "&" key on a typewriter, meaning "and."
store: Abundance or plenty.
larks: Singing birds.
imp: Attach.
affliction: Hardship or struggle.

Epitaphs

PLAY TRACK 34

Here lies the body of our Anna
Done to death by a banana.
It wasn't the fruit that laid her low
But the skin of the thing that made her go.

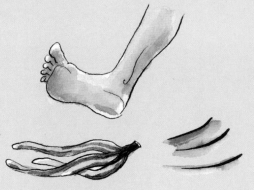

PLAY TRACK 35

Here lies
Lester Moore
Four slugs
from a .44
no Les
no More.

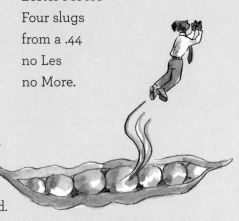

PLAY TRACK 36

Here under this **sod** and under these trees
Is buried the body of Solomon Pease.
But here in this hole lies only his pod;
His soul is shelled out and gone up to God.

PLAY TRACK 37

Within this grave do lie,
Back to back, my wife and I;
When the last **trump** the air shall fill,
If she gets up, I'll just lie still.

PLAY TRACK 38

Pause, stranger, when you pass me by.
For as you are, so once was I.
As I am now, so will you be.
Then prepare unto death, and follow me.

If You're a Poet, You Should Know It

alphabet poem: A poem that's arranged so that readers follow through every letter of the alphabet, from A to Z.

riddle poem: A poem, usually short, with a puzzle hidden inside.

shaped poem: A poem whose line length and structure are arranged carefully so that the poem's shape on the page adds to the meaning.

epitaph: An inscription carved on a tombstone.

Words for the Wise

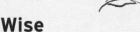

sod: Dirt.
trump: Short for "trumpet."

PART TWO

Poetry's Greats:
Rulers of Rhyme, Legends of the Lyric,
and Superstars of the Spoken Word

THE FIRST POET
Homer • c. 700–800 BC

Thousands of years ago, a poet in Greece wrote about the great war stories of his day in two epic poems: *The Iliad* (pronounced "ILL-ee-ad") and *The Odyssey* (pronounced "ODD-iss-ee"). That poet was Homer, and those epic poems are the oldest works in the history of poetry. Though there were surely other poets before Homer, none of their writings survived.

Not much is known about him, but Homer was rumored to have been a blind poet who spent his life wandering through Greece and entertaining people with his poems some time around 700 or 800 BC (That means about 2,750 years ago!)

The Iliad told of the story of a warrior named Achilles (pronounced "uh-KILL-eez") and the battle to win the Greek city of Troy. *The Odyssey* was its sequel and described the journey of Greek soldier Odysseus (pronounced "oh-DISS-ee-us") back to his home after the war for Troy ended.

μὲν γάρ

Because he lived so long ago, we hardly know anything about Homer. Some people think he never existed at all. Others think *The Iliad* and *The Odyssey* were actually written by two different people. Still others think that Homer might have been a woman. No one knows for sure.

Did we mention epics are long? *The Iliad* runs over fifteen thousand lines!

from THE ILIAD

by Homer

The **Wrath** of Peleus Son, O Muse, **resound**;
Whose **dire** Effects the Grecian Army found:
And many a Heroe, King, and hardy Knight,
Were sent, in early Youth, to Shades of Night:
Their Limbs a **Prey** to Dogs and Vulturs made;
So was the **Sov'reign Will** of Jove obey'd:
From that ill-**omen'd** Hour when **Strife** begun,
Betwixt Atrides Great, and Thetis God-like Son.

—translated by John Dryden

Words for the Wise

wrath: Furious anger.
resound: Echo loudly.
dire: Disastrous.
prey: Something hunted for food.
sov'reign will: A god's right to have things happen as he or she wants (from an old-fashioned spelling of "sovereign").
omen: A sign of things to come.
strife: Hardship and war.

➧ PLAY TRACK 39

The Iliad was originally written in Greek—Homer's language—and has been translated into many other languages since then. This passage was translated by the seventeenth-century British poet John Dryden. It is the introduction setting the stage for the long and bloody tale that is to come.

In it, the poet warns us that we're about to hear of the wrath of Peleus's son (Achilles) on the Grecian (or Greek) army. It's a violent tale, he says, where many are sent to their deaths—to "Shades of Night."

The Greeks had many gods, including the supreme god, Jove, and they believed events happened according to the gods' wishes. "So was the Sov'reign Will of Jove obey'd," the poem tells us. In other words, "We can thank the gods for all the fighting!" The story begins at the cursed, or "ill-omen'd," hour when bad blood erupts between the sons of Atrides ("uh-TREE-dees") and Thetis ("THEE-tis")—Agamemnon ("ag-uh-MEM-non") and Achilles, the two rivals at the beginning of *The Iliad*.

THE BARD
William Shakespeare • 1564–1616

Homer may have been the first poet, but no writer in history—before or since—wrote verse that was more beautiful than William Shakespeare's.

Shakespeare wrote dozens of plays—sometimes three a year—and more than 150 poems.

As with many of the poets from long ago, little is known about Shakespeare's life. We do know that as a kid growing up in Stratford-on-Avon in England, he likely would have seen many plays performed. These were days long before television, and live actors performing in outdoor theaters were the closest things people had to the movies.

Shakespeare went to work as a young man to help support his family and was married at age eighteen. When he was twenty-one, he headed to London. There he began working in the theater as an actor and writer. His plays won praise from nearly everyone who saw them.

Shakespeare's plays can be thought of as long poems. He wrote his lines with careful attention to their length—often with ten syllables in each line—and sometimes used rhyming words at the end.

It may not have been exactly how people talked in real life, but it was how plays were written in his day. And Shakespeare was a master at it. The beautiful language in his plays flowed smoothly from one word to the next, and hearing one of his plays being performed is like listening to a beautiful poem in many voices.

No one knows for sure why Shakespeare left Stratford-on-Avon at the age of twenty-one. Some say he was going to help England fight Spain. Some think he left to become a country schoolteacher. Others say he was forced to leave after he killed a deer on a nobleman's property: the nobleman got angry, and Shakespeare skipped town to avoid punishment. Whatever Shakespeare's reasons for leaving, we're all lucky he did, because it was in London that he began his career as a writer.

from MACBETH

by William Shakespeare

Double, double, toil and trouble,
Fire burn and cauldron bubble.

Fillet of a fenny snake,
In the cauldron boil and bake;
Eye of newt, and toe of frog,
Wool of bat, and tongue of dog,
Adder's fork, and blindworm's sting,
Lizard's leg, and howlet's wing—
For a charm of pow'rful trouble,
Like a hell-broth boil and bubble.

Double, double, toil and trouble,
Fire burn and cauldron bubble . . .

Cool it with a baboon's blood,
Then the charm is firm and good.

◆► PLAY TRACK 40

Shakespeare's play *Macbeth*, written around 1606, is filled with ghosts, witches, and other spooks. The story tells of a Scottish nobleman who plots to become king through murder and treachery. During the play, he seeks advice from a fearsome crew of witches. Here, they list off the ingredients as they brew one of their evil potions.

Words for the Wise

cauldron: A big, black pot (the type used by witches to stir up trouble).

fillet: A thin slice of meat.

fenny: Dirty, or something that comes from the ground.

newt: A small, lizard-like amphibian.

Adder's fork: The forked tongue of an adder snake.

howlet: A young owl.

Shakespeare would become the most admired writer of his day. His plays were blockbusters, and when he turned to writing poetry later in life, he wrote sonnets that are considered as fine as any poems ever composed in that difficult form.

After his incredible success in London, Shakespeare returned to his hometown of Stratford-on-Avon, where he retired from writing. He died in 1616 at age fifty-two, but his work lives on in plays and poems that are performed and recited every day around the world.

Many of Shakespeare's plays were performed at the Globe Theater in London. It was a great place to see a play. The theater had eight sides and the audience sat in a circle around the stage, so anywhere you sat you had a terrific view.

Unlike many other poets who gained fame after their death, Shakespeare became a star during his own lifetime—and made loads of money.

Sonnet 30

by William Shakespeare

When to the sessions of sweet silent thought
I summon up remembrance of things past,
I sigh the lack of many a thing I sought,
And with old **woes** new **wail** my dear time's waste:

Then can I drown an eye, unused to flow,
For precious friends hid in death's dateless night,
And weep afresh love's long since cancelled woe,
And moan th' expense of many a vanished sight.

Then can I grieve at grievances **foregone**,
And heavily from woe to woe tell o'er
The sad account of **fore-bemoaned** moan,
Which I new pay as if not paid before.

But if the while I think on thee, dear friend,
All losses are restored and sorrows end.

In the first quatrain, the poet describes how he becomes sad when he looks back on his failures—"the lack of many a thing I sought."

In the next quatrain, he remembers lost loves and friends who have died, which brings enough tears to "drown an eye."

In the third quatrain, he describes how his old losses still seem new to him now—"from woe to woe tell o'er . . . Which I new pay as if not paid before."

But in the final couplet, the poet is reminded of a true, dear friend, and that comforting thought is enough to wipe away all the sadness. (That's some friend, huh?)

Words for the Wise

woe: Trouble and heartache.
wail: A sad and lonely cry.
foregone: Something that is already over and done with.
fore-bemoaned: Old-fashioned language for something that has already been cried over.

A MAN OF MANY (MANY, MANY) WORDS

Shakespeare's plays are filled with characters that recite his poems through their lines. Many of these lines have become famous poems in their own right. **Do you recognize any of these?**

If we shadows have offended,
Think but this, and all is mended—
That you have but slumb'red here
While these visions did appear.

The fairy Puck, begging the audience's pardon and reminding them that it was all just a dream, from A Midsummer Night's Dream

All that **glisters** is not gold;
Often have you heard that told.

The prince of Morocco, reading words found on a scroll, from The Merchant of Venice

Sigh no more, ladies, sigh no more!
Men were **deceivers** ever,
One foot in sea, and one on shore;
To one thing constant never.

The prince's assistant Balthasar, joking about how men cannot be trusted, from Much Ado about Nothing

Good night, good night! Parting is such sweet sorrow
That I shall say good night till it be morrow.

Juliet bidding Romeo good night, from Romeo and Juliet

Where the bee sucks, there suck I;
In a **cowslip**'s bell I lie;
There I **couch** when owls do cry.
On the bat's back I do fly
After summer merrily.
Merrily, merrily, shall I live now
Under the blossom that hangs on the bough.

The fairy Ariel, describing her tiny nature, from The Tempest

Words for the Wise
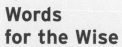

deceivers: Liars and cheaters.
glisters: Sparkles like glitter.
cowslip: A yellow or purple flower.
couch: Hide.

THE FREE SPIRIT
John Milton • 1608–1674

John Milton was a spirited poet who followed his own rules at a time when most people who hoped to be successful followed a strict path. Rather than becoming a lawyer or a priest as his family wished, he chose to study literature.

He grew up in England, and by the age of thirty, he had already become a respected poet. When many English citizens complained they were mistreated by King Charles and demanded more freedoms, Milton championed their causes in his writings. His work sometimes got him into hot water with the authorities, and he even spent some time in jail.

During the last decade of his life, Milton turned from writing about current events and instead focused on grand themes like religion and the meaning of life (heavy stuff—but it's full of beautiful poetic passages). This was the time when he slowly composed his great masterpieces, including *Paradise Lost*—an epic poem that is often compared with Homer's *The Iliad* and *The Odyssey*. Milton died in 1674 and is considered, along with Homer and Shakespeare, one of the greatest writers in history.

Milton thought that *Paradise Lost* was too serious a poem to contain rhymes. Instead, he used **blank verse**, which describes a poem with a careful structure but no rhyming. In the case of *Paradise Lost*, that meant every line had to have ten syllables.

If You're a Poet, You Should Know It

blank verse: Poems that contain no rhymes but have rules about line length and structure.

By age fifty, Milton was totally blind. To write his poems, he would recite them to his daughters, who would dutifully (though sometimes grumpily) write down everything he said.

from PARADISE LOST

by John Milton

With thee **conversing** I forget all time,
All seasons and their change, all please alike.
Sweet is the breath of **morn**, her rising sweet,
With charm of earliest Birds; pleasant the Sun
When first on this delightful Land he spreads
His **orient** Beams, on herb, tree, fruit, and flow'r,
Glist'ring with dew; fragrant the fertile earth
After soft showers; and sweet the coming-on
Of grateful Ev'ning mild, then silent night,
With this her solemn Bird and this fair Moon,
And these the Gems of Heav'n, her starry train:
But neither breath of Morn when she **ascends**
With charm of earliest Birds, nor rising Sun
On this delightful land, nor herb, fruit, flow'r,
Glist'ring with dew, nor fragrance after showers,
Nor grateful Evening mild, nor silent Night
With this her solemn Bird, nor walk by Moon,
Or glittering Starlight without thee is sweet.

Words for the Wise

conversing: Speaking.
morn: Morning.
orient: Dazzling and bright.
ascends: Climbs.

🎧 **PLAY TRACK 42**

Published in 1667, Milton's *Paradise Lost* is considered the greatest epic poem ever written in the English language. It was inspired by the story of Adam and Eve from the Bible and what is called the "fall from grace"—the moment when sin was introduced into the world.

In the passage above, Eve describes her love for Adam and how when they speak, it's as if the rest of the world doesn't exist: "With thee conversing, I forget all time."

She describes the changing of the seasons, birds singing at dawn, the moon shining in the night—all the beauty of the natural world—but then adds that none of these wonders would mean anything to her if she were to experience them alone: "Neither breath of Morn . . . nor rising Sun . . . nor silent Night . . . nor walk by Moon . . . without thee is sweet."

THE ARTIST
William Blake • 1757–1827

William Blake was an artist. He was born in England in 1757, but unlike many other poets of his time, he was not educated in religion and literature. Instead, he was sent to drawing school. Later, he worked as an apprentice to an engraver who carved images into metal plates. The plates were then used to print books.

This experience, combined with a powerful imagination and a deep love of the natural world, would be all the tools Blake would need to create his beautiful verse. He combined art and poetry in illustrated books he produced himself. He wrote vivid poems about the wonder of nature and the problems of modern life, and drew detailed pictures that he printed alongside them. For some of his books, he and his wife painted each page by hand, so no two were exactly alike. Blake considered his art and his poetry inseparable—one would not be complete without the other.

Though he only experienced success for a short time as a poet, Blake remained dedicated to his poetry. Money may have been tight at times, but he never gave up his craft. He continued writing poems until he died at age seventy.

Blake had a wild and brilliant imagination even as a child. Some might say too wild—he claimed to have seen God through a window and angels in the trees outside.

Blake called his method of combining poems and visual art "illuminated printing," or casting light upon words. In this case, the "light" was the understanding that the drawings added to his poetry.

Laughing Song

by William Blake

When the green woods laugh, with the voice of joy
And the **dimpling** stream runs laughing by,
When the air does laugh with our merry **wit**,
And the green hill laughs with the noise of it.

When the meadows laugh with lively green
And the grasshopper laughs in the merry scene,
When Mary and Susan and Emily,
With their sweet round mouths sing Ha, Ha, He.

When the painted birds laugh in the shade
Where our table with cherries and nuts is spread
Come live & be merry and join with me,
To sing the sweet chorus of Ha, Ha, He.

⏵• PLAY TRACK 43

William Blake's most famous work was a collection of poems entitled *Songs of Innocence and of Experience*, which he published in 1794. Like many poets, Blake used the word "song" to mean poem. We know "innocent" to mean someone who has done nothing wrong, and Blake used "songs of innocence" to describe poems about the beauty of gentle animals, children, and nature. His songs of "experience," on the other hand, showed the struggles and hardships of society—the world in which we all live.

The poem "Laughing Song" comes from *Songs of Innocence*. In the first two stanzas, the forest is described as a happy and carefree place where even streams and grasshoppers can be heard giggling, and where children—"Mary and Susan and Emily"—join in the fun. In the third stanza, the poem suggests that grown-ups might be wise to follow their lead. In the woods, where life is simple, everyone smiles.

Words for the Wise

dimpling: Something with lots of ups and downs on its surface (like the water in a brisk stream).
wit: Sense of humor.

THE PEOPLE'S POET
William Wordsworth • 1770–1850

William Wordsworth is remembered as the poet of the everyday man and woman, a writer who changed the rules about poetry by striving to make it something everyone could enjoy.

As a boy growing up in England in the late nineteenth century, Wordsworth was an average student who gave little hint of the acclaimed poet he would become. But in his late twenties, Wordsworth began to focus on writing poetry and worked closely with his friend and fellow poet Samuel Taylor Coleridge. In 1798, the two published a collection called *Lyrical Ballads*. It was a huge change from the poetry that had come before.

Instead of the carefully crafted poems filled with fancy words, *Lyrical Ballads* featured poems that were meant to be read by everyone, not just the highly educated. "Men speaking to men," Wordsworth called it. He and Coleridge wrote about nature but in a realistic way that wasn't afraid to show the grit and the grime, too. Inspired by the French and American Revolutions, they wrote about liberty and the rights of all people. This new style became known as **Romanticism**. Wordsworth continued writing throughout his life, publishing many poems and essays. He died at age eighty.

While traveling in France as a young man, Wordsworth fell in love with a woman and the two had a daughter, Caroline. But money problems forced Wordsworth to go home to England. After war broke out between England and France, he wouldn't be able to return to France for ten years. Ten years was too long a time for the couple to be apart, and they never followed through with their plans to marry.

If You're a Poet, You Should Know It

Romanticism: Poetry filled with the spirit of nature, freedom, and the imagination, and written to be enjoyed by everyone.

Romanticism isn't what you think... No Kissing!

I Wandered Lonely as a Cloud

by William Wordsworth

I wandered lonely as a cloud
That floats on high o'er **vales** and hills,
When all at once I saw a crowd,
A host, of golden daffodils;
Beside the lake, beneath the trees,
Fluttering and dancing in the breeze.

Continuous as the stars that shine
And twinkle on the **milky way**,
They stretched in never-ending line
Along the **margin** of a bay:
Ten thousand saw I at a glance,
Tossing their heads in **sprightly** dance.

The waves beside them danced; but they
Outdid the sparkling waves in **glee**:
A poet could not but be gay,
In such a **jocund** company;
I gazed—and gazed—but little thought
What wealth the show to me had brought:

For **oft**, when on my couch I lie
In **vacant** or in **pensive** mood,
They flash upon that inward eye
Which is the bliss of solitude;
And then my heart with pleasure fills,
And dances with the daffodils.

Words for the Wise

vales: Valleys.
milky way: The galaxy of stars that includes our sun.
margin: Edge.
sprightly: Lively and with energy.

glee: Giddy happiness.
jocund: Jolly.
oft: Often.
vacant: Empty, lonely.
pensive: Thoughtful.

◄◄ PLAY TRACK 44

In "I Wandered Lonely as a Cloud," written in 1804, William Wordsworth describes the visual brilliance of a field of flowers, and how the scene comforted him at a time when he was lost and lonesome. Later, when he's feeling blue—"In vacant or in pensive mood"—he thinks back to that scene and smiles: "my heart with pleasure fills."

The poem is beautifully simple and hardly needs explaining—which is just the way Wordsworth wanted it to be.

DAUGHTER, WIFE, POET
Elizabeth Barrett Browning • 1806–1861

Though she never had a formal education, Elizabeth Barrett Browning was the most famous woman poet of her day. She was born in England in 1806 and began writing at a young age. She was barely a teenager when her father had some of her first work published.

Browning struggled with her health nearly all her life and spent most of her time sick at home with her ten brothers and sisters. But that gave her plenty of time to read and write. Her father was incredibly strict, refusing to allow any of his children to marry, and Elizabeth continued writing from her family home. By age forty, she was a widely respected poet and writer. She once wrote nice things about the poems of another writer, Robert Browning. He was so pleased by what she'd said that he tracked her down to thank her. Though he was six years younger than she, the two fell in love. Against her father's wishes, they married and moved to Italy.

Together, Robert and Elizabeth Barrett Browning spent many happy years writing. Her strength improved after she moved out of her family's home, but she never fully regained her health. She died in 1861, and her husband lived for nearly thirty years after her death. He never remarried.

After being thrown from a pony when she was fifteen, Elizabeth Barrett Browning was so badly injured that she was forced to lie on her back for years afterward. It kept her from going to school—but not from becoming a famous writer.

◆◆ PLAY TRACK 45

In the mid-1840s, Elizabeth Barrett Browning wrote her collection *Sonnets from the Portuguese* to express the deep love she felt for her husband. The collection contains forty-four poems altogether, and "Sonnet 43" has become the most well known.

Browning's words are packed with meaning and can sometimes be a little hard to understand. But if you remember that each line is part of the description of how strong her love is, it's not so tough to follow.

The poem has become one of the most famous expressions of love ever written.

Sonnet 43
from *Sonnets from the Portuguese*

by Elizabeth Barrett Browning

How do I love thee? Let me count the ways.
I love thee to the depth and breadth and height
My soul can reach, when feeling out of sight
For the ends of Being and ideal Grace.

I love thee to the level of everyday's
Most quiet need, by sun and candle-light.
I love thee freely, as men strive for Right;
I love thee purely, as they turn from Praise.

I love thee with the passion put to use
In my old griefs, and with my childhood's faith.
I love thee with a love I seemed to lose
With my lost saints—I love thee with the breath,

Smiles, tears, of all my life!—and, if God choose,
I shall but love thee better after death.

In the opening quatrain, Browning describes how her love reaches the limits of all possible feeling—"to the depth and breadth [or width] and height / My soul can reach . . ." It extends beyond what even seems possible, she says, "out of sight / For the ends of Being and ideal Grace."

In the next quatrain, she tells how she adores her beloved for all the little things—"everyday's / Most quiet need," and that she loves "freely" and "purely." It's almost like she's reciting wedding vows.

The third quatrain shows that the power of her love is as strong as any feelings she has ever felt, even anger or sadness—"the passions put to use / In my old griefs . . ." It's even stronger than a child's faith in God, she says—"I love thee with a love I seemed to lose / With my lost Saints— . . ."

In the touching final two-line couplet, Browning says that her love will never end—"if God choose, / I shall but love thee better after death."

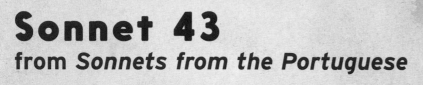

A POET OF "FANTASTIC TERRORS"
Edgar Allan Poe • 1809–1849

When it comes to spookiness, no other poet can match Edgar Allan Poe. He wrote poems and stories filled with weird characters, creepy ghosts, peculiar animals, and other strange goings-on. In his poem "The Raven," he speaks of "fantastic terrors"—a phrase that just about sums up his work.

It's not hard to see why Edgar Allan Poe wrote about such dark things. When he was only three and living in Virginia, his mother died, and his father died a short time after that. The Poe children were separated, and Edgar ended up being raised by the Allan family (that's where he got his middle name). Though he received a good education both in England and America, Poe did not get along well with his adoptive parents, and he left for Boston to make his own way in the world at around age eighteen.

From then on, he lived the rough life of a writer, never having much money and quickly spending whatever he earned. Poe traveled much between Virginia, Baltimore, and New York, and he was married until his young wife died at age twenty-four. All the while, he wrote fabulous poems and stories that made him famous but never made him rich. He was engaged to be married again when his hard life of poverty and sickness finally caught up with him. He died in 1849 at age forty.

◄► PLAY TRACK 46

Poe's most famous poem, "The Raven," published in 1845, is a fine example of what made Poe's writing so special. The subject is creepy enough—a mysterious bird that arrives in the night. But it's the language he uses that makes the poem a classic.

Many of the lines contain *internal rhyme*—rhyming words within the same line—like "weary" and "dreary" in the poem's first line. And Poe's words seem to dance off the tongue through his use of *alliteration*—words that start with the same letter—like "nodded, nearly napping" in the third line. The poem is rich with symbolism, too—references to scary places and things that add to the spooky mood.

"The Raven" is told from the viewpoint of the *narrator*. "I stood there wondering, fearing, / Doubting," he says. It's as if the narrator were grabbing us by the collar and saying, "This happened to me!"

All this contributes to the suspense that builds throughout "The Raven," just like in a detective story or scary movie. The language races to the finish, and you can almost feel the poet's heart beating faster and faster each time the Raven cries, "Nevermore!"

The Raven

by Edgar Allan Poe

Once upon a midnight dreary, while I **pondered**, weak and weary,
Over many a **quaint** and curious volume of forgotten **lore**—
While I nodded, nearly napping, suddenly there came a tapping,
As of some one gently rapping, rapping at my chamber door.
"'tis some visitor," I muttered, "tapping at my chamber door—
     Only this, and nothing more."

 The **narrator** (or the person telling the story) describes a dark and lonely night as he sits in his study, hoping his books will bring him some comfort from the misery he's felt ever since losing his beloved Lenore, the young woman who stole his heart. He is disturbed by the knock at his door and finally goes to see who's there.

Deep into that darkness peering, long I stood there wondering, fearing,
Doubting, dreaming dreams no **mortal** ever dared to dream before;
But the silence was unbroken, and the stillness gave no **token**,
And the only word there spoken was the whispered word, "Lenore?"
Then I whispered, and an echo murmured back the word "Lenore!"
     Merely this and nothing more.

 The narrator is puzzled but decides the sound must be the wind. He returns inside, only to hear a tapping at the window.

Open here I flung the shutter, when, with many a flirt and flutter
In there stepped a **stately** Raven of the **saintly days of yore**;
Not the least **obeisance** made he; not a minute stopped or stayed he;
But, with **mien** of lord or lady, perched above my chamber door—
Perched upon a bust of Pallas just above my chamber door—
     Perched, and sat, and nothing more.

 A dark, mysterious bird flies inside and lands on the "bust of Pallas" (a statue of a Greek god from the neck up). The Raven acts like it is a king, hardly noticing the man inside. When the narrator asks its name, the Raven replies, "Nevermore."

The Raven (continued)

But the Raven, sitting lonely on the **placid** bust, spoken only
That one word, as if his soul in that one word he did outpour.
Nothing farther then he **uttered**—not a feather then he fluttered—
Till I scarcely more than muttered, "Other friends have flown before—
On the **morrow** he will leave me, as my Hopes have flown before."
                    Then the bird said, "Nevermore."

 When he asks when the bird will leave him—as his other friends have left—
its reply is "Nevermore." Growing angry, the narrator asks when his sorrow
over the lost Lenore will end. "Nevermore," the Raven replies. Will Lenore
find peace in Heaven, the narrator asks, his temper rising. "Nevermore" is
the answer. The poet jumps to his feet and orders the Raven to return to
whatever dark place he came from—"the tempest [or furious storm] and
the Night's Plutonian shore! [the dark underworld of the Greek gods]."

"Be that word our sign of parting, bird or fiend!" I shrieked, **upstarting**—
"Get thee back into the **tempest** and the Night's Plutonian shore!
Leave no black plume as a token of that lie thy soul hath spoken!
Leave my loneliness unbroken!—quit the bust above my door!
Take thy beak from out my heart, and take thy form from off my door!"
                    Quoth the Raven, "Nevermore."

And the Raven, never flitting, still is sitting, still is sitting
On the **pallid** bust of Pallas just above my chamber door;
And his eyes have all the **seeming** of a demon's that is dreaming,
And the lamp-light o'er him streaming throws his shadow on the floor;
And my soul from out that shadow that lies floating on the floor
                    Shall be lifted—nevermore!

Words for the Wise

pondered: Was sitting and thinking.
quaint: Old-fashioned.
lore: Stories from long ago.
mortal: A living person.
token: A hint or clue.
stately: Dignified and proper.
saintly days of yore: The olden days.
obeisance: A bow or curtsy.
mien: Attitude or appearance.
placid: Calm and quiet.

uttered: Spoke in a low voice.
morrow: Tomorrow.
upstarting: To jump up.
tempest: A violent storm, like a hurricane.
plume: A feather.
quoth: Says (a fancy way of saying "quotes").
pallid: Pale white.
seeming: Appearance.

If You're a Poet, You Should Know It

internal rhyme: Words within the same line of the poem that rhyme.
alliteration: Stringing words together that start with the same letter or sound.
narrator: The speaker in a poem or story.

A REBEL WITHOUT APPLAUSE
Emily Dickinson • 1830–1886

Since her death, many have said that Emily Dickinson was the greatest American poet. But they didn't say that during her lifetime. In fact, almost no one had even heard of her or her poems when she was still alive—which was just the way she wanted it.

As poets go, Emily Dickinson was an oddball. She spent most of her life hidden away in her Massachusetts home writing

With just a few exceptions, Emily Dickinson never left Amherst, Massachusetts; in fact, she hardly ever left her house!

poems that she kept stuffed inside her desk. She wrote *her* poems in *her* style for *herself*, and aside from a few friends, no one knew about her amazing skills as a poet. Other poets sought fame and fortune, but not Emily Dickinson. She was a rebel.

Emily Dickinson was born in 1830 and grew up in a strictly religious family, as was usual in those days. It is thought that sometime during her early twenties, she fell hopelessly in love with someone—though it's not clear exactly with whom, or why the love affair fell apart. But we do know her heart was broken. For the rest of her life, she stayed in her family home, writing her moving—though often sad— poems, alone in her room.

Emily Dickinson wrote her poems (close to two thousand all together) on any scrap of paper she could find.

Dickinson is known for poems that express deep, powerful feelings in just a few, carefully selected words. Long poems containing lots of fancy language were popular at that time. But Dickinson blazed her own trail by writing simple poems on grand themes like loneliness and love.

After she died at age fifty-five, her sister found the poems Emily had stuffed inside her desk. They were soon published, and Emily Dickinson became a star. But she never knew it—and she wouldn't have cared.

➡◆ PLAY TRACK 48

In what is probably Emily Dickinson's most famous poem, "Because I Could Not Stop for Death," she writes about a theme that many think of when they think of Dickinson: death. The spooky poem begins with Death as a carriage driver who picks the narrator up when her life is over. She says she's not ready to go—"I could not stop for Death"—but he was ready for her—"He kindly stopped for me."

On the way, her life passes before her eyes. In the third stanza they see a school, a scene from her childhood. Then they pass a wheat field, where adults work. Then they look upon a sunset representing the end of the day, and the end of life.

The narrator admits that death is frightening and compares that fear to a chill. In the fourth stanza, she's cold because the thin clothes she's wearing provide little warmth. Then they pass a house that is almost completely buried in the ground—just like a grave. The final stanza describes how the ride goes on forever, "toward Eternity.

➡◆ PLAY TRACK 47

In "I'm nobody! Who are you?" Emily Dickinson expresses her carefree attitude toward fame. "I'm nobody!" she announces proudly in the first line, as if to say, "I don't have fame—and I don't want it!" She reaches out to us by asking, "Are you—Nobody—too?" and reminds us that we don't have to be famous to be special.

She even makes fun of what it must be like to be a celebrity, comparing it to being a frog in a swamp endlessly croaking to all the other frogs. "How dreary—to be—Somebody!" she says—pretty appropriate words for a writer who kept her own poems in a drawer, hidden from the world.

I'm nobody! Who are you?

by Emily Dickinson

I'm nobody! Who are you?
Are you—Nobody—Too?
Then there's a pair of us?
Don't tell!
They'd advertise—you know!

How dreary—to be—Somebody!
How public—like a Frog—
To tell one's name—the livelong June—
To an admiring Bog!

Words for the Wise

advertise: Make something public.
dreary: Dark, cold, and miserable.
bog: A wet, swampy area.

Because I Could Not Stop for Death

by Emily Dickinson

Because I could not stop for Death—
He kindly stopped for me—
The Carriage held but just Ourselves—
And **Immortality**.

We slowly drove—He knew no **haste**
And I had put away
My labor and my leisure too,
For His **Civility**—

We passed the School, where Children **strove**
At Recess—in the Ring—
We passed the Fields of Gazing Grain—
We passed the Setting Sun—

Or rather—He passed Us—
The Dews drew quivering and chill—
For only **Gossamer**, my Gown—
My **Tippet**—only **Tulle**—

We paused before a House that seemed
A Swelling of the Ground—
The Roof was scarcely visible—
The **Cornice**—in the Ground—

Since then—'tis Centuries—and yet
Feels shorter than the Day
I first **surmised** the Horses' Heads
Were toward Eternity—

Words for the Wise

immortality: Infinity and the afterlife.
haste: Hurry.
civility: Kindness and good manners.
strove: Competed or played.
gossamer and **tulle:** Thin fabrics.
tippet: A scarf.
cornice: Decoration along a house's rooftop.
surmised: Realized.

VOICE OF AMERICA
Walt Whitman • 1819–1892

Walt Whitman led the charge in America during the nineteenth century to write poetry that could be understood and enjoyed by everyone, poems of freedom that celebrated the common man. His voice was the voice of America.

Whitman was born in New York in 1819. As a member of a large, poor family, he didn't receive much education, and he tried many things without much luck while he was still a young man, including running a newspaper, working as a

schoolteacher, and writing bad poetry. When he was thirty-six, Whitman published *Leaves of Grass*, a book of poetry he hoped would be enjoyed not only by scholars but by everyone. He rejected the stuffy poetry of old and wrote fresher, freer verse in much the same way that Romantic poets in England, like William Wordsworth, had.

At first critics called his writing rude, crude, and worthless. But little by little, they caught on. Whitman eventually became a widely respected poet in both America and Europe, though, as with many poets, his writings never made him rich. He continued writing poems throughout his life and died at the age of seventy-two.

During the Civil War, Walt Whitman worked as a nurse at a military hospital, tending to the wounded, reading to them during their long recoveries, and helping them write letters home.

This is no book; Who touches this, touches a man.

—*Walt Whitman, describing the power of poetry in his books*

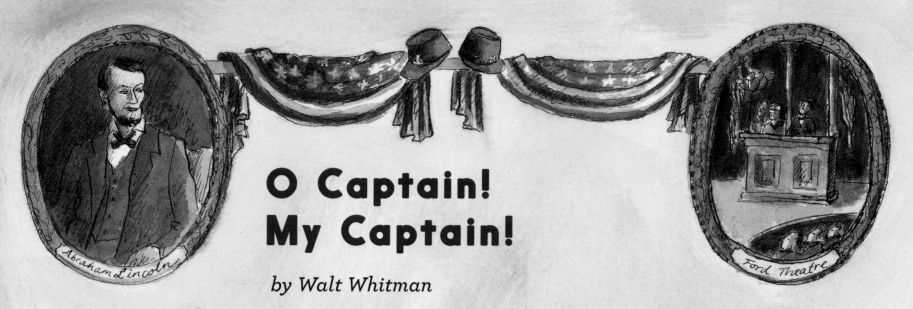

O Captain! My Captain!

by Walt Whitman

O Captain! my Captain! our fearful trip is done,
The ship has weather'd every **rack**, the prize we sought is won,
The port is near, the bells I hear, the people all **exulting**,
While follow eyes the steady **keel**, the **vessel** grim and daring;
　　　But O heart! heart! heart!
　　　　　O the bleeding drops of red,
　　　　　　　Where on the deck my Captain lies,
　　　　　　　　　Fallen cold and dead.

O Captain! my Captain! rise up and hear the bells;
Rise up—for you the flag is flung—for you the bugle **trills**,
For you bouquets and ribbon'd wreaths—for you the shores a-crowding,
For you the call, the swaying mass, their eager faces turning;
　　　Here Captain! dear father!
　　　　　This arm beneath your head!
　　　　　　　It is some dream that on the deck,
　　　　　　　　　You've fallen cold and dead.

My Captain does not answer, his lips are pale and still,
My father does not feel my arm, he has no pulse nor will,
The ship is anchor'd safe and sound, its voyage closed and done,
From fearful trip the victor ship comes in with object won;
　　　Exult O shores, and ring O bells!
　　　　　But I with mournful **tread**,
　　　　　　　Walk the deck my Captain lies,
　　　　　　　　　Fallen cold and dead.

●→ PLAY TRACK 49

Walt Whitman became a great admirer of President Abraham Lincoln during the Civil War.

After Lincoln was shot and killed in Ford's Theater in Washington, DC, in 1865, Whitman wrote "O Captain! My Captain!" in the president's honor.

The poem compares Lincoln to the captain of a ship who has successfully steered his vessel through dangerous waters, just as the president led the nation through the Civil War. But Lincoln has been assassinated, and the captain cannot celebrate the victory—"his lips are pale and still."

Whitman's use of symbolism—likening the death of the nation's president to the death of a ship's captain—captured the sorrow felt by many upon Lincoln's death.

Words for the Wise

rack: Violent shaking.
exulting: Loudly celebrating.
keel: A plank along the bottom of a boat that adds stability.
vessel: Boat or ship.
trills: Notes blown one after the other.
tread: A slow, heavy-footed walk.

A POET OF HEAVEN AND EARTH
Christina Rossetti • 1830–1894

Christina Rossetti was destined for stardom. Her talented family included a famous professor (her father, Gabriele), a renowned painter and poet (her brother Dante Gabriel), and respected writers who wrote about art and literature (her sister, Maria Francesca, and brother William Michael).

Rossetti was born in London, England, in 1830. Like many women in her day, she received most of her education at home, where, in addition to her lessons, she was able to soak up knowledge and culture from her other family members and from the many visitors who came to see her father.

Though two different admirers asked for her hand in marriage, Rossetti never accepted their proposals. She was deeply religious, and it is thought that Rossetti felt neither of the men was devoted enough to God.

Instead of becoming a wife, Rossetti focused on being a writer and, later, on the volunteer work she performed for religious charities. Many of her poems were about religion, but she also wrote beautiful sonnets, fanciful ballads, and somber poems about love and death. Her most famous poem is "Goblin Market," a ballad beloved by children as an enchanting fable and debated by scholars for its tricky symbolism. Rossetti died in 1894, a few weeks after her sixty-fourth birthday.

Christina Rossetti grew more religious as she grew older. One book she particularly admired included a line that said "God is evil," so she taped a slip of paper over it. That way, she could enjoy the book without feeling guilty!

As a poet, Christina Rossetti started young. Before the age of twelve, she presented her mother with a birthday poem she'd written, "To My Mother." (That's something to think about next time Mother's Day rolls around . . .) Rossetti's grandfather later had the poem privately published.

THREE POEMS BY CHRISTINA ROSSETTI

Boats Sail on the Rivers

Boats sail on the rivers,
    And ships sail on the seas;
But clouds that sail across the sky
    Are prettier far than these.

There are bridges on the rivers,
    As pretty as you please;
But the bow that bridges heaven,
    And overtops the trees
And builds a road from earth to sky,
    Is prettier far than these.

Who Has Seen the Wind?

Who has seen the wind?
    Neither I nor you:
But when the leaves hang trembling
    The wind is passing **thro'**.

Who has seen the wind?
    Neither you nor I:
But when the trees bow down their heads
    The wind is passing by.

What Is Pink?

What is pink? a rose is pink
By the fountain's **brink**.
What is red? a **poppy**'s red
In its barley bed.
What is blue? the sky is blue
Where the clouds float thro'.
What is white? a swan is white
Sailing in the light.
What is yellow? pears are yellow,
Rich and ripe and mellow.
What is green? the grass is green,
With small flowers between.
What is violet? clouds are violet
In the summer twilight.
What is orange? why, an orange,
Just an orange!

●❖ PLAY TRACKS 50, 51, and 52

Rossetti spent most of her life in the crowded city of London. But as a girl, she loved to play outdoors on visits to her grandparents' country home.

She never forgot those adventures. Years later, Rossetti captured the memories in her spirited children's poems. "Boats Sail on the Rivers" insists that a cloud floating in the sky is prettier than any ship floating in the sea. "Who Has Seen the Wind?" marvels at the invisible power of the blowing breeze. In "What Is Pink?" she catalogs the colors by rummaging through nature's box of crayons.

Words for the Wise

thro': An old-fashioned way of saying "through."
brink: The edge or rim of something.
poppy: A colorful flower.

POEMS OF EVERYDAY BEAUTY
Robert Frost • 1874–1963

Robert Frost is celebrated for the simple beauty of his poetry and his ability to write about ordinary things—farms, workers, animals—in a way that casts them in an extraordinary light. His poems hint at the wonder that sometimes hides behind everyday things.

Frost was born in San Francisco and moved to New England when he was ten. He graduated from high school, got married, spent a few years in college, and dreamed of becoming a professional poet. But, like many writers throughout history, Frost found that

poetry doesn't always get your bills paid. (And it didn't help that he was writing plain poems about ordinary things at a time when big words and fancy styles were popular.)

After trying many different jobs, Frost moved his family to England. There, he met other poets, submitted his work to a publisher, and soon had his first collection on the shelves at bookstores. His

writing career took off almost immediately. When he returned to the United States a few years later, he was a star.

From then on, Frost was able to live his dream of a life dedicated to poetry. His beautiful, uncomplicated verse about life in America was praised by scholars and loved by ordinary people. He died in 1963 at the age of eighty-eight.

In 1961, Robert Frost performed the great honor of reciting a poem at the inauguration of President John F. Kennedy.

He received many, many awards and many honorary degrees from universities across the country. He won the Pulitzer Prize—the highest honor awarded to an American poet—four times. Frost is the only writer ever to have done so.

The Road Not Taken

by Robert Frost

Two roads diverged in a yellow wood,
And sorry I could not travel both
And be one traveler, long I stood
And looked down one as far as I could
To where it bent in the undergrowth;

Then took the other, as just as fair,
And having perhaps the better claim,
Because it was grassy and wanted wear;
Though as for that the passing there
Had worn them really about the same,

And both that morning equally lay
In leaves no step had **trodden** black.
Oh, I kept the first for another day!
Yet knowing how way leads on to way,
I doubted if I should ever come back.

I shall be telling this with a sigh
Somewhere ages and ages **hence**:
Two roads diverged in a wood, and I—
I took the one less traveled by,
And that has made all the difference.

Words for the Wise

trodden: Worn by the passage of many feet.
hence: Since then.

➡️ PLAY TRACK 53

Published in 1915, Robert Frost's "The Road Not Taken" is a tribute to the individual and to everyone who has ever gone against the grain to do what they think is right.

The two paths Frost describes in the opening stanza are symbols of the decisions we often must make in life. The poet admits he's "sorry I could not travel both." But he's just "one traveler" and therefore must choose one path.

Though the two paths look almost the same, one seems a bit less used—"it was grassy and wanted wear," he says in the second stanza. It's the road that fewer people have taken, so that's the path he follows. The other route has been chosen more often and is likely the easier journey. But life isn't about taking the easy way, the poem reminds us; it's about going where your heart and mind lead you.

Frost hints that he's using the road as a symbol, as something that stands for much more than just a woody path, in the final sentence, which adds, "And that has made all the difference." The poet has followed his own heart throughout his life and doesn't regret for a second where it has taken him.

THE ADVENTURER
Robert Louis Stevenson • 1850–1894

Born a sick child in 1850, Robert Louis Stevenson only lived to the age of forty-four. But he made the most of it.

Stevenson attended school like most boys growing up in Edinburgh, Scotland, and by the age of twenty-five, he had become a lawyer. Shortly after receiving his degree, however, he hit the road. In Stevenson's day, doctors often advised patients who had long been suffering from disease to seek warmer climates and fresher air, and Stevenson took this advice to heart. He traveled the world from Scotland to America to Tahiti to Australia, and to many places in between. Though he never completely outran his illness, he experienced a wide variety of peoples and lifestyles that he wrote about in his poems, stories, and novels, including *Treasure Island* and *Dr. Jekyll and Mr. Hyde*.

But he wasn't known only for stories of suspense on the high seas or of men turning into monsters. Stevenson was a respected poet, and his classic collection, *A Child's Garden of Verses*, has been reprinted and re-illustrated countless times since.

Stevenson died suddenly on a December day in 1894 while on an island in the South Pacific, working on a book. The next day, natives buried him atop a tall mountain peak overlooking the sea. It was just as he'd wished.

 EXCERPTS

Under the wide and starry sky
Dig the grave and let me lie;
Glad did I live and gladly die,
    And I laid me down with a will.

This be the verse you grave for me:
Here he lies where he longed to be;
Home is the sailor, home from the sea,
    And the hunter home from the hill.

Robert Louis Stevenson wrote these words as a set of instructions to be carried out after he died. The final three lines are carved on the marker above his grave.

Sing me a song of a lad that is gone,
Say, could that lad be I?
Merry of soul he sailed on a day
Over the sea to Skye.

    —*Robert Louis Stevenson,*
    from Songs of Travel

Words for the Wise
Skye: An island off the coast of Scotland.

Windy Nights

by Robert Louis Stevenson

Whenever the moon and stars are set,
        Whenever the wind is high,
All night long in the dark and wet,
        A man goes riding by.
Late in the night when the fires are out,
Why does he gallop and gallop about?

Whenever the trees are crying aloud,
        And ships are tossed at sea,
By, on the highway, low and loud,
        By at the gallop goes he.
By at the gallop he goes, and then
By he comes back at the gallop again.

◄◆ PLAY TRACK 54

"Windy Nights" was published in 1885 in Stevenson's *A Child's Garden of Verses*. The eerie evening described in the poem, with wind that cries through the trees and tosses ships at sea, becomes spookier still when the mysterious nighttime rider arrives.

"Why does he gallop and gallop about?" the poet wonders, and the words are written with a rhythm that almost gallops off the tongue—much like the up-and-down clip-clopping of a horse passing by at breakneck speed.

AN ENGLISHMAN IN BOMBAY
Rudyard Kipling • 1865–1936

Born in Bombay, India, Rudyard Kipling was a British writer who captured the feel and flavor of Indian life in his many books, short stories and poems. His writings for children and adults included novels of high adventure and imaginative stories about the lives of wild animals.

Kipling lived in India until age six, when he was sent off to his family's homeland of England. Once he arrived, he was put in the strict care of a relative while his parents remained in India—and he was miserable. He was happier after he was sent away to boarding school at age twelve, and he later wrote about his friends and adventures there in his book *Stalky and Co.*

After his schooling Kipling returned to India, where he became a journalist and began writing stories and poems. He traveled to Japan, England, San Francisco, New York, and Vermont. He was married in 1892 and later had three children. In 1894, he published the first part of *The Jungle Book*, stories about a boy growing up among wild animals that would become his most famous work. Kipling spent much of his later years in England, where he continued writing up until his death in 1936.

His poems were enjoyed by everyday people and were widely praised for their thoughtful messages, interesting characters, and rhymes that looked easy but were anything but easy to write.

Rudyard Kipling was named after Rudyard Lake in Staffordshire, England, where his parents first met.

◗◆ PLAY TRACK 55

Rudyard Kipling's "If" was published in 1910, and is an inspirational poem about the lessons of life.

The poem is a single, 288-word sentence that touches on a wide array of the challenges that may arise as you make your way in the world. Your patience will be tested. Others might tell lies about you. You may lose your fortune. You might see things you've built fall apart. But, the poet writes, if you can rise to these challenges, keep a cool head, and learn from your experiences, you will grow into a good person.

Kipling's message is one that has been told by wise men and women for centuries, but the familiar examples and his gentle rhymes make it much more than the typical lesson about doing the right thing. And though Kipling addresses his poem to boys ("you'll be a Man, my son!" he says), his words are universal. The encouraging message about honesty, fairness, and kindness applies to boys, girls, and all people.

If *by Rudyard Kipling*

If you can keep your head when all about you
    Are losing theirs and blaming it on you,
If you can trust yourself when all men doubt you,
    But make allowance for their doubting too;
If you can wait and not be tired by waiting,
    Or being lied about, don't deal in lies,
Or being hated, don't give way to hating,
    And yet don't look too good, nor talk too wise;

If you can dream—and not make dreams your master;
    If you can think—and not make thoughts your aim;
If you can meet with Triumph and Disaster
    And treat those two imposters just the same;
If you can bear to hear the truth you've spoken
    Twisted by **knaves** to make a trap for fools,
Or watch the things you gave your life to, broken,
    And stoop and build 'em up with worn-out tools;

If you can make one heap of all your winnings
    And risk it on one turn of **pitch-and-toss**,
And lose, and start again at your beginnings
    And never breathe a word about your loss;
If you can force your heart and nerve and **sinew**

To serve your turn long after they are gone,
And so hold on when there is nothing in you
    Except the Will which says to them: "Hold on!"

If you can talk with crowds and keep your virtue,
    Or walk with Kings—nor lose the common touch,
If neither foes nor loving friends can hurt you,
    If all men count with you, but none too much;
If you can fill the unforgiving minute
    With sixty seconds' worth of distance run,
Yours is the Earth and everything that's in it,
    And—which is more—you'll be a Man, my son!

Words for the Wise

knaves: Dishonest people.
pitch-and-toss: A form of gambling played by tossing coins.
sinew: Body tissue that connects to muscles.

A GOOD POET FOR BAD CHILDREN
Hilaire Belloc • 1870–1953

Hilaire Belloc (pronounced "hill-AIR" "BELL-ock") was successful at a wide range of pursuits, but he said that if he could be remembered for one thing, he hoped it would be his poetry. He got his wish.

Belloc's fantastically silly poems for the young and the young at heart are collected in books to which he gave outlandish titles, like *The Bad Child's Book of Beasts* and *More Beasts for Worse*

Children. Today, that might not seem so shocking. But Belloc was writing his wickedly clever rhymes a hundred years ago, back when such nonsense was frowned upon—especially by grown-ups!

Belloc was born outside Paris, France, in 1870 and spent much of his childhood in England. He published some of his first poems while he was a teenager working at a newspaper.

Later, he was an excellent student at England's finest schools, then he became a tutor and professor. He wrote many books and essays on topics of the day, as well as serious

poetry. But it is the lighthearted children's poetry for which he is famous. He lived a long, productive writer's life and died in 1953.

Hilaire Belloc got around. He was born in France, went to school in England, and taught classes in America. Later, he was a member of the House of Commons (a branch of British government) in London.

Hilaire Belloc was famous for the curious titles he gave to his work. One poem he called "Jim, Who Ran Way from His Nurse, and Was Eaten by a Lion."

Two Poems by Hilaire Belloc

The Frog

Be kind and tender to the Frog,
    And do not call him names,
As "Slimy skin," or "Polly-wog,"
    Or likewise "Ugly James,"
Or "Gap-a-grin," or "Toad-gone-wrong,"
    Or "Bill Bandy-knees":
The Frog is justly sensitive
    To epithets like these.

No animal will more repay
    A treatment kind and fair;
At least, so lonely people say
Who keep a frog (and, by the way,
They are extremely rare).

The Vulture

The Vulture eats between his meals,
    And that's the reason why
He very, very rarely feels
    As well as you and I.

His eye is dull, his head is bald,
    His neck is growing thinner.
Oh! what a lesson for us all
    To only eat at dinner!

Words for the Wise

justly: Understandably.
epithets: Bad words or unpleasant nicknames.

➡ PLAY TRACKS 56 and 57

Hilaire Belloc's silly poems for children poked fun at the boring nursery rhymes that good boys and girls were expected to read at the time. Just as parents today frown at some of the things kids bring home, parents a hundred years ago often turned up their noses at Belloc's rhymes.

But his poems have stood the test of time. The characters were clever and sassy—and often got what was coming to them. Belloc also wrote about animals, with a devilish insight shared by few writers before or since. Here, in a poem published in 1896, he describes a frog who is sensitive to name-calling, and in a poem published a year later, he describes a vulture who pays the price for overeating.

AMERICAN SPIRIT
Carl Sandburg • 1878–1967

Carl Sandburg was a champion of the American spirit. He wrote about famous Americans who had done great things and not-so-famous Americans whose achievements were on a smaller scale. He captured the beauty of the landscape and wrote about the determination of its people. Sandburg thought America was a special place, and he spent his life expressing that in his poems, songs, and books.

Born in a small Illinois town in 1878, Sandburg went to school until only the eighth grade. After that, he worked at odd jobs, traveled trains as a hobo, joined the army, and became a newspaper reporter. At night, he worked on his own writing. Sandburg met his wife after moving to Chicago, a city that would be the subject of some of his earliest poems.

He soon had his first poems published and began working on a biography of Abraham Lincoln. Scholars and ordinary readers alike praised his work, and before long he was one of the best-loved writers in America. He died in 1967 at the age of eighty-nine.

Carl Sandburg's biography of Abraham Lincoln took him thirty years to write and ran six books long. Sandburg thought Lincoln was the model of the American hero.

Carl Sandburg was a man of many talents—at poetry readings, he would often pull out his guitar and play folk songs!

Buffalo Dusk

by Carl Sandburg

The buffaloes are gone.
And those who saw the buffaloes are gone.
Those who saw the buffaloes by thousands and
      how they pawed the prairie **sod** into dust
      with their hoofs, their great heads down
      pawing on in a great pageant of dusk,
Those who saw the buffaloes are gone.
And the buffaloes are gone.

🔊 PLAY TRACK 58

In "Buffalo Dusk," published in 1948, Carl Sandburg remembers the great crowds of wild buffalo that once lived on the American frontier but were hunted nearly to extinction. The poem is sad and reminds us that we lost something forever when the wild buffalo died out. Sandburg also reminds us that not only are the buffalo gone, the memory of them is nearly gone, too. No one is alive today who ever witnessed the great herds that once wandered the plains. If we're not careful, the poem cautions, soon we'll have forgotten the buffalo altogether. And then what might be next to go?

Words for the Wise

sod: Dirt and grass.

It is thought that there were once perhaps 70 million buffalo roaming the American plains. (If there were still that many buffalo around today, there would be enough for every American family to have one as a pet!) But between 1800 and 1900, hunters almost completely wiped them out. By the turn of the century, there were only a few hundred left in the wild. Today, their surviving descendants are protected on farms and nature preserves.

Theme in Yellow

by Carl Sandburg

I spot the hills
With yellow balls in autumn.
I light the prairie cornfields
Orange and tawny gold clusters
And I am called pumpkins.
On the last of October
When dusk is fallen
Children join hands around me
Singing ghost songs
And love to the harvest moon;
I am a jack-o'-lantern
With terrible teeth
And the children know
I am fooling.

◆→ PLAY TRACK 59

In "Theme in Yellow," Carl Sandburg playfully paints his canvas in the colors of autumn through his description of a field glowing with orange and gold.

In simple free verse, Sandburg uses a technique called **personification** as he pretends to be a pumpkin: "I spot the hills," he says, describing the large, round pumpkins that dot the landscape in autumn. Poets use personification to give human life to objects—animals, vegetables, rocks, or anything else—which allows us to understand these objects in a new way. Here, Sandburg's personification of a pumpkin lets us hear what a pumpkin might be thinking as Halloween approaches.

The poet slyly refers to the annual celebration of spooks when he describes the events that take place on "the last of October," when he becomes a jack-o'-lantern and bares his "terrible teeth," much to the delight of the children dancing around him. It's all a game, of course: "the children know I am fooling."

If You're a Poet, You Should Know It

personification: A technique used by writers to give human qualities to nonhuman objects.

THE THINKER
W. H. Auden • 1907–1973

Wystan Hugh Auden was one of the great poetic minds of the twentieth century. He came from a smart and well-to-do family and studied a wide array of subjects in school. As a poet, he wrote in just about every form of poetry under the sun—villanelles, pastorals, ballads, and free verse, among many others. His poems ranged from the fun and simple to the incredibly complex, and his subjects included everything from love to politics. He was truly a writer who could do it all.

Auden was born in England in 1907 and went to college in Oxford to study to become an engineer. But he soon found

his true calling was poetry. After graduating, he traveled in Germany. His first book of poetry, called *Poems*, was published in 1930.

Auden became a teacher in Scotland, continued writing, and married Erika Mann, the daughter of German writer Thomas Mann, in 1935. Auden received the King's Gold Medal for Poetry in 1937, then left for the United States, which, apart from a few brief jobs as a visiting professor at Oxford, would be his home for the rest of his life.

As Auden's reputation grew, he accepted teaching jobs at many colleges in America's Northeast, and spent much of his time as a member of New York City's community of writers. He shared a deep affection with Chester Kallman, a writer

with whom he spent much time and who helped Auden with his own work. Auden became a U.S. citizen in 1946 and continued writing poems, plays and books about poetry until his death in 1973.

W. H. Auden is honored in the "Poets' Corner" section of Westminster Abbey in London. Some of Great Britain's most famous writers are buried there, including Geoffrey Chaucer (one of England's first poets), Rudyard Kipling, and Robert Browning. Others, like John Milton, William Wordsworth, and Dylan Thomas have plaques dedicated to them there.

🔊 PLAY TRACK 60

W. H. Auden wrote "Night Mail" in 1935. The poem describes the trip the mail made as it journeyed overnight between the cities of Euston and Glasgow in Scotland. The details—birds turning their heads at the noise, a jug rattling on a bed stand as the train passes, letters with pictures drawn in the margins—appear in stark contrast to the powerful engine speeding through the night loaded with messages of every kind.

The eight stanzas that make up the first part of the poem are written in a steady rhythm that brings to mind the chugging of a locomotive as it climbs the Scottish hills. In the poem's second part, Auden switches to an easy, flowing free verse as he describes the train's glide downhill into the city of Glasgow. He compares the bustling city there to the peacefulness of the countryside, describing the busy machinery as "a glade of cranes" and "fields of apparatus."

Words for the Wise

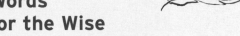

glade: An open, grassy space.
apparatus: A combination of machinery.
glens: Small valleys.
lochs: Scottish term for lakes.
situations: Another word for "jobs."
circumstantial: Detailed, but not necessarily important.

Night Mail *by W. H. Auden*

I

This is the Night Mail crossing the Border,
Bringing the cheque and the postal order,

Letters for the rich, letters for the poor,
The shop at the corner, the girl next door.

Pulling up Beattock, a steady climb:
The gradient's against her, but she's on time.

Past cotton-grass and moorland border,
Shovelling white steam over her shoulder,

Snorting noisily, she passes
Silent miles of wind-bent grasses.

Birds turn their heads as she approaches,
Stare from bushes at her blank-faced coaches.

Sheep-dogs cannot turn her course;
They slumber on with paws across.

In the farm she passes no one wakes,
But a jug in a bedroom gently shakes.

II

Dawn freshens. Her climb is done.
Down towards Glasgow she descends,
Towards the steam tugs yelping down a **glade** of cranes,
Towards the fields of **apparatus**, the furnaces
Set on the dark plain like gigantic chessmen.
All Scotland waits for her:
In dark **glens**, beside pale-green **lochs**,
Men long for news.

III

Letters of thanks, letters from banks,
Letters of joy from girl and boy,
Receipted bills and invitations
To inspect new stock or to visit relations,
And applications for **situations**,
And timid lovers' declarations,
And gossip, gossip from all the nations,
News **circumstantial**, news financial,
Letters with holiday snaps to enlarge in,
Letters with faces scrawled in the margin,
Letters from uncles, cousins, aunts,
Letters to Scotland from the South of France,
Letters of condolence to Highlands and Lowlands,
Written on paper of every hue,
The pink, the violet, the white and the blue,
The chatty, the catty, the boring, the adoring,
The cold and official and the heart's outpouring,
Clever, stupid, short and long,
The typed and the printed and the spelt all wrong.

IV

Thousands are still asleep,
Dreaming of terrifying monsters
Or a friendly tea beside the band in Cranston's or Crawford's:
Asleep in working Glasgow, asleep in well-set Edinburgh,
Asleep in granite Abberdeen,
They continue their dreams,
But shall wake soon and hope for letters,
And none will hear the postman's knock
Without a quickening of the heart.
For who can bear to feel himself forgotten?

(Track 60 continued)
Auden switches back to rhyming verse for the third part of the poem. This fast-paced passage describes the many different types of mail the train carries—from bills and bank statements to love letters and notes filled with "holiday snaps" (or vacation pictures).

The fourth and final part of the poem returns to the wandering free verse as it imagines the many people who will receive the letters, all still fast asleep. Few people think of the journey the mail makes until it arrives at the doorstep, the poem tells us. And no one knows what the mail will bring—or if it will bring anything at all. But, of course, with "a quickening of the heart," everyone hopes the postman or woman will bring something. Auden's poem describes the wonder of the everyday, the amazing goings-on behind the scenes that are seldom thought of but that mean so much to so many.

A BRAVE NEW VOICE
Langston Hughes • 1902–1967

Langston Hughes was the first successful African American poet, and he paved the way for the many black writers who would follow. He wrote about life as a black man in the United States and the often unequal treatment African Americans received. He was living at a time when discussing things like that could get someone into trouble—but he wrote about them anyway.

Hughes was born in Missouri and traveled throughout America and Europe, both with his family and later on his own. He lived for a time in the Harlem section of New York City and became a leading voice of the Harlem **Renaissance**—the period when black art and music began to gain acceptance in America. He began writing poetry and was soon recognized as a talented writer who captured the spirit of black America as no writer had before.

Hughes wrote many poems that dealt with race. But he was also the author of numerous books, plays, and children's poetry that celebrated life, nature, the bustle of the city, and many other ideas. He died in New York in 1967.

Some of Langston Hughes's poems captured, for the first time in writing, the spirit of the songs of hardship that had been sung by black Americans for generations—the blues.

I got the blues...

Words for the Wise

Renaissance: A period of rapid and exciting growth in arts and culture.

To make words sing is a wonderful thing.

—Langston Hugh[

In Time of Silver Rain

by Langston Hughes

In time of silver rain
The earth
Puts forth new life again,
Green grasses grow
And flowers lift their heads,
And over all the plain
The wonder spreads
      Of life,
      Of life,
      Of life!

In time of silver rain
The butterflies
Lift silken wings
To catch a rainbow cry,
And trees put forth
New leaves to sing
In joy beneath the sky
As down the roadway
Passing boys and girls
Go singing, too,
In time of silver rain
      When spring
      And life
      Are new.

⏩ PLAY TRACK 61

Langston Hughes's poem "In Time of Silver Rain" describes the power of a spring rainfall to bring new life after the cold winter months. In the first stanza, he describes grasses and flowers as if they were waking up from a long sleep. In the second stanza, butterflies, trees—even boys and girls—lift their heads to sing in celebration of the cool spring rains.

{ For children who wondered why poets write their poems, Hughes offered this answer: "If you put your thoughts in rhyme, they stay in folks' heads a longer time." }

THE BEAT OF THE CITY
Lawrence Ferlinghetti • 1919–

Lawrence Ferlinghetti was a leader of the Beat Generation—a group of writers, artists, musicians and other free spirits in the 1950s and '60s. The Beats, as they were called, made it a point to be different, to go their own way and to try new things. The Beats rebelled against authority, believing that people should have the freedom to do what they want, as long as it doesn't hurt others.

Jack Kerouac, another famous Beat writer, defined the Beat Generation as "down and out but full of intense conviction"—meaning they were exhausted from dealing with life (they were "beat") but full of big ideas and determined to express them.

Some complained that this was a silly, childish attitude. But others saw it as a courageous new way of looking at modern life. The best work of the Beats had an energy and a spirit that was unlike any other poetry before it.

Ferlinghetti was born in New York and lost his family at an early age. His father died before he was born, and shortly afterward his mother was sent to a hospital for the mentally ill. As a boy, Ferlinghetti moved around among homes. He later joined the Navy, and studied in North Carolina, New York, and France before moving with his wife to San Francisco.

There, he and a partner opened a bookstore called City Lights Books. It became a meeting place for poets and artists, and it also published many Beat writers' books, including Ferlinghetti's own work.

Ferlinghetti writes wild free verse in a unique style that captures the freedom

and spirit of the Beats. His poems often take on unusual structures. For example, in his poem "Fortune," he scatters words all over the page. Though his poems might not look like what we're used to, Ferlinghetti has a special ability to capture the way people talk. His poems are at their best when read aloud.

Fortune   *by Lawrence Ferlinghetti*

Fortune

              has its cookies to give out

which is a good thing

              since it's been a long time since

       that summer in Brooklyn

      when they closed off the street

      one hot day

        and the

            FIREMEN

                    turned on their hoses

and all the kids ran out in it

      in the middle of the street

and there were

        maybe a couple dozen of us

              out there

with water squirting up

         to the

           sky

             and all over

               us

there was maybe only six of us

           kids altogether

running around in our

          barefeet and birthday

  suits

      and I remember Molly but then

the firemen stopped squirting their hoses

     all of a sudden and went

        back in

        their firehouse

        and

started playing **pinochle** again

     just as if nothing

     had ever

     happened

while I remember Molly

        looked at me and

 ran in

because I guess really we were the only ones there

◄► PLAY TRACK 62

Lawrence Ferlinghetti's "Fortune" appeared in his book *Coney Island of the Mind*, a hugely successful collection published in 1958. The poem looks back on a summer day in the city when firemen turned on their water hoses to give neighborhood kids a break from the heat. Like many of the memories we have from long ago, the poet can't quite recall everything about the day. At first, he remembers dozens of kids, then "maybe only six." In the end, it's just him and his friend Molly. He might get the details mixed up, but he remembers the important stuff—like dancing in the refreshing spray of the firemen's hoses.

Words for the Wise

pinochle: A popular card game.

IRISH EYE
Seamus Heaney • 1939–2013

Seamus Heaney (pronounced "SHAY-muss" "HEE-knee") is known for his moving, straightforward poetry about life in Northern Ireland, poems that make us think about our own lives and the big world around us.

He was born in 1939 in Northern Ireland, a section of Ireland that remained a part of Great Britain after the rest of the island gained its independence. Heaney grew up on a farm and was a good student. He joined a poets' group in college and went on to become a teacher after graduating. In 1965 he got married and in 1966 published his first book of poetry, *Death of a Naturalist*. The book was praised as a great work, and soon people were saying that Heaney was the next great Irish writer.

After that, he taught as a professor at many colleges in Europe and the United States, published numerous books, and received lots of awards.

Like many writers, Seamus Heaney was also a big reader. The first book he ever owned was the adventure novel *Kidnapped*, by Robert Louis Stevenson, who wrote the poem "Windy Nights."

➦ PLAY TRACK 63

Seamus Heaney's poem "Digging" was published in his 1966 book, *Death of a Naturalist*, and is a gentle tribute to his family's history. At the same time, it makes us think about the violent history of Northern Ireland—the Protestants have fought to remain part of Great Britain while the Catholics have struggled for independence.

The poet describes watching his father in the garden digging up potatoes—a crop grown by Irish farmers for centuries. It seems like his father has been doing this forever, the poet tells us, and he watches as his father "bends low, comes up twenty years away." It's a scene the young observer has seen many times before. His grandfather grew potatoes, too, and the poet tells us his father shovels "just like his old man." The poet remembers bringing his grandfather a bottle of milk to drink, then watching him go right back to digging, just as his father does now.

But the poet himself won't be a digger. He's a writer. Instead of digging into the earth with a shovel, he'll write about the land with his pen. He holds it tightly between his fingers—"snug as a gun," he says in the first stanza, like the guns many Irish have used in their history of fighting. But instead of a shovel, or a gun, the poet uses a pen: "I'll dig with it."

Digging

by Seamus Heaney

Between my finger and my thumb
The squat pen rests; snug as a gun.

Under my window, a clean **rasping** sound
When the spade sinks into gravelly ground:
My father, digging. I look down

Till his straining rump among the flowerbeds
Bends low, comes up twenty years away
Stooping in rhythm through potato drills
Where he was digging.

The coarse boot nestled on the lug, the shaft
Against the inside knee was **levered** firmly.
He rooted out tall tops, buried the bright edge deep
To scatter new potatoes that we picked,
Loving their cool hardness in our hands.

By God, the old man could handle a **spade**.
Just like his old man.

My grandfather cut more turf in a day
Than any other man on Toner's bog.
Once I carried him milk in a bottle
Corked sloppily with paper. He straightened up
To drink it, then fell to right away
Nicking and slicing neatly, heaving sods
Over his shoulder, going down and down
For the good turf. Digging.

The cold smell of potato mould, the squelch and slap
Of soggy peat, the **curt** cuts of an edge
Through living roots awaken in my head.
But I've no spade to follow men like them.

Between my finger and my thumb
The squat pen rests.
I'll dig with it.

Words for the Wise

rasping: A high-pitched scraping sound.
levered: Positioning an object against something else to make it easier to move.
spade: A shovel.
nicking: Making thin cuts.
curt: Short and sharp.

> With phrases like "spade sinks into gravelly ground," "curt cuts," and "squelch and slap," Seamus Heaney uses alliteration to mimic the sound a shovel might make as it digs into the ground and tosses aside piles of dirt.

VISIONS OF MEXICO
Octavio Paz • 1914–1998

Europe and America aren't the only places that have produced masterful poets. Writers of beautiful verse have come from countries all around the world.

Octavio Paz was born in 1914 and grew up in a family with little money in an old, rundown house on the outskirts of Mexico City. "As rooms collapsed, we moved the furniture into another," Paz once said. He published his first poem when he was only seventeen, and he would continue writing for the rest of his life. Along with his poems, he wrote essays on freedom and local political topics. Later he would travel to America, a country much richer and in many ways more advanced than Mexico. He captured these differences in his writings, wondering about the good and the bad of two countries that seemed to be opposites.

But Paz was a writer of curiosity and imagination, too, and perhaps nowhere do these qualities shine as brightly as in his story "My Life with the Wave." The tale tells of a boy who takes a wave home as a pet after a visit to the beach—and of the adventures that follow. "If I caught and hugged her," the boy says, "She would rise up tall like a liquid tree, then burst into a shower and bathe me in her foam."

Paz married in 1964, and as he continued writing and traveling, he grew to be a greatly respected figure. He served as a college professor, an ambassador, and a magazine editor, and he received many honors and awards. He died in 1998.

Octavio Paz didn't like to follow the traditional rules of writing. Sometimes his work was half essay, half poem. One poem had parts written in four different languages!

Octavio Paz received the Nobel Prize in Literature in 1990.

The Street

by Octavio Paz

A long and silent street.
I walk in blackness and I stumble and fall
and rise, and I walk blind, my feet
stepping on silent stones and dry leaves.
Someone behind me also stepping on stones, leaves:
if I slow down, he slows;
if I run, he runs. I turn: nobody.
Everything dark and doorless.
Turning and turning among these corners
which lead forever to the street
where nobody waits for, nobody follows me,
where I pursue a man who stumbles
and rises and says when he sees me: nobody.

➥ PLAY TRACK 64

Octavio Paz's creepy poem "The Street" was published in the 1940s. Paz wrote the poem in his native Spanish, and the poet Muriel Rukeyser translated it into English.

The poem describes stumbling through the darkness on a strange and unfamiliar street. Worse, the narrator is being followed by someone who copies his every move. "I slow down, he slows; / if I run, he runs," the poem tells us. But when he turns to see who's there: "nobody."

The catch comes in the final few lines. The narrator adds that he, too, is following someone—someone who turns around and sees no one, just as when he looks for his own pursuer. And he lets us in on the secret: "nobody follows me," the narrator admits, as if it's all been in his head. He's been chasing his own shadow all along.

The poem brings to mind the eerie feeling of wandering in search of something we'll never find. We fool ourselves into thinking we might catch it, but we know, deep down, that we never will. Quite a message for what seemed like such a simple poem, isn't it?

CAGED BIRD'S SONG
Maya Angelou • 1928–2014

Maya Angelou (pronounced "MY-a" "AN-ja-loo") has become one of the public's favorite poets, and as a successful black woman, she is widely admired as an inspiration for women, African Americans, and anyone who has ever stood up in the face of a challenge.

Angelou's life story is a tale of achievement over hardship—just like the themes of some of her most famous poems. She was born in St. Louis, Missouri, in 1928, but she spent much of her childhood living with her grandmother in Arkansas. It was a time when black people in the South were treated very differently than white people, and Angelou would describe these hard times later in her books and poems.

While still a teenager, she moved to California and gave birth to a baby boy. There, she fought for equality for black people and struggled to provide for herself and her son. She worked at many different jobs in many different places and published *I Know Why the Caged Bird Sings*, the first part of the story of her life, in 1970. Later, she wrote more books about her life and several collections of poetry. She was a popular speaker and a college professor.

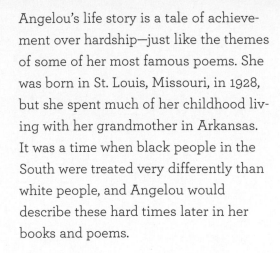

Maya Angelou was more than a famous poet—she appeared on television, starred in movies, danced in musicals, and performed in plays.

When President Bill Clinton was sworn into office, Maya Angelou recited a special poem she had written for the occasion. It was only the second time a poet had ever been asked to read at a presidential inauguration. (The first was when Robert Frost read for John F. Kennedy in 1961.)

Life Doesn't Frighten Me

by Maya Angelou

Shadows on the wall
Noises down the hall
Life doesn't frighten me at all
Bad dogs barking loud
Big ghosts in a cloud
Life doesn't frighten me at all.

Mean old Mother Goose
Lions on the loose
They don't frighten me at all
Dragons breathing flame
On my counterpane
That doesn't frighten me at all,

I go boo
Make them shoo
I make fun
Way they run
I won't cry
So they fly
I just smile
They go wild
Life doesn't frighten me at all.

Tough guys in a fight
All alone at night
Life doesn't frighten me at all.
Panthers in the park
Strangers in the dark
No, they don't frighten me at all.

That new classroom where
Boys all pull my hair
(Kissy little girls
With their hair in curls)
They don't frighten me at all.

Don't show me frogs and snakes
And listen for my scream,
If I'm afraid at all
It's only in my dreams.

I've got a magic charm
That I keep up my sleeve,
I can walk the ocean floor
And never have to breathe.
Life doesn't frighten me at all
Not at all
Not at all.
Life doesn't frighten me at all.

⏵● PLAY TRACK 65

Perhaps none of Maya Angelou's poems better expresses her pride, her spirit, her fearlessness, and her determination than "Life Doesn't Frighten Me," which was published in her 1978 book, *And Still I Rise*.

The poem is a bold announcement that she refuses to be frightened by anything. Barking dogs, ghosts, shadows, dragons, frogs, and snakes have no power to scare this poet. In fact, she scares them back! "I go boo / Make them shoo," Angelou writes. And it's not just spooks and ferocious animals. "Kissy little girls" and "tough guys" can't rattle her, either.

In a world that has its share of troubles to toss at you—many of which Angelou has battled during her own life—she's proud to say that she's a survivor.

GLOSSARY

alliteration: Stringing words together that start with the same letter or sound.

alphabet poem: A poem that's arranged so that readers follow through every letter of the alphabet, from A to Z.

anonymous: The term used for the author of a poem when the original writer is unknown.

ballad: A poem that tells a short story in a moving and exciting way.

blank verse: Poems that contain no rhymes but have rules about line length and structure.

climax: The high point of a poem after the tension has built up, and where the action that will change everything occurs. (A climax in a poem is just like a climax in a movie, when the hero squares off with the bad guy for the final showdown.)

couplet: A stanza made up of two lines.

epitaph: An inscription carved on a tombstone.

free verse: A style of poetry with no set length or rhyme scheme; its only rule is that it has no rules.

haiku: A short poem of three lines and seventeen syllables describing nature and often a particular time of year.

idealistic: Fanciful or not very grounded in real life.

internal rhyme: Words within the same line of a poem that rhyme.

limerick: A short, humorous, five-line poem.

lyric verse: A broad classification for poems that are shorter than narrative poems and describe feelings and emotions.

narrative verse: A story told in the form of a poem. The word "narrative" comes from narrator—one who tells stories. "Verse" is another word for poetry.

narrator: The speaker in a poem or story.

nonsense verse: A type of poetry featuring fantastic images or made-up words that entertains through its wild silliness.

nursery rhymes: Fun, usually short poems written for children and often recited at bedtime.

pastoral: A lyric verse about shepherds, nature, or country living.

personification: A technique used by writers to give human qualities to nonhuman objects.

quatrain: A stanza made up of four lines.

rhyme scheme: The way the words that rhyme are arranged within a poem.

riddle poem: A poem, usually short, with a puzzle hidden inside.

Romanticism: Poetry filled with the spirit of nature, freedom, and the imagination, and written to be enjoyed by everyone.

Shakespearean sonnet: A fourteen-line poem made up of three quatrains and a couplet.

shaped poem: A poem whose line length and structure is arranged carefully so that the poem's shape on the page adds to the meaning.

stanza: The way lines are grouped together, like paragraphs, within a poem.

structure: The way a poem is organized. Usually this means how long the poem is, how many lines are in each stanza, and whether or not words rhyme.

supernatural: Eerie things that come from beyond and that cannot be easily explained.

syllable: Individual parts of a word, like beats in a musical measure. "Cat" has one beat, or one syllable. "Basket" has two syllables: bas-ket. "Superman" has three syllables: su-per-man.

symbol: An image selected by a writer to represent something else, like "light" meaning "life," or "dark" meaning "death."

triplet: A stanza made up of three lines.

verse: Another word for poetry.

villanelle: A nineteen-line poem with a careful rhyme scheme.

BIBLIOGRAPHY

Ackroyd, Peter. *T. S. Eliot*. New York: Simon and Schuster, 1984.

Allison, Alexander W., et al., eds. *The Norton Anthology of Poetry,* 3rd ed. New York: W. W. Norton & Company, 1970.

Angelou, Maya. *And Still I Rise*. New York: Random House, 1978.

Belloc, Hillaire. *Cautionary Verses*. New York: Knopf, 1941.

Birkhead, Edith. *Christina Rossetti and Her Poetry*. London: The Folcroft Press, 1930.

Blake, William. *The Complete Poems*. Edited by Alicia Ostriker. New York: Penguin, 1977.

Brandreth, Gyles Daubeney. *Famous Last Words and Tombstone Humor*. New York: Sterling, 1979.

Buckley, Jerome Hamilton, and George Benjamin Woods, eds. *Poetry of the Victorian Period,* 3rd ed. New York: HarperCollins, 1965.

Carroll, Lewis. *Through the Looking Glass and What Alice Found There*. New York: Harper & Bros., 1902.

Coffman, Ramon P., and Nathan G. Goodman. *Famous Authors for Young People*. New York: Dodd, Mead & Company, 1943.

Cohen, Gary. "A Notorious Trifler." *The Atlantic Monthly,* July/August 2002, 110.

Cummings, E. E. *Tulips and Chimneys*. New York: Liveright, 1976.

Daringer, Helen Fern, and Anne Thaxter Eaton, eds. *The Poet's Craft*. New York: Harcourt, Brace & Wood, 1935.

Deutsch, Babette. *The Poetry Handbook: A Dictionary of Terms*. New York: Funk & Wagnalls, 1969.

Dickinson, Emily. *Final Harvest: Emily Dickinson's Poems*. New York: Little, Brown and Company, 1961.

Eliot, T. S. *Old Possum's Book of Practical Cats*. New York: Harcourt Brace Jovanovich, 1967.

Ferlinghetti, Lawrence. *Pictures of the Gone World,* 2nd ed. San Francisco: City Lights Books, 1995.

Foerster, Norman. *American Poetry and Prose*. Boston: Houghton Mifflin, 1934.

Fuller, John. *W. H. Auden: A Commentary*. Princeton, NJ: Princeton University Press, 1998.

Goring, Rosemary, ed. *Larousse Dictionary of Writers*. New York: Larousse Kingfisher Chambers Inc., 1994.

Hamilton, Ian. The Oxford Companion to Twentieth-Century Poetry in English. Oxford: Oxford University Press, 1994.

Hass, Robert, ed. *The Essential Haiku: Versions of Basho, Buson, and Issa*. Hopewell, NJ: The Ecco Press, 1994.

Heaney, Seamus. *Opened Ground: Selected Poems*. New York: Farrar, Straus and Giroux, 1998.

Hughes, Langston. *The Collected Poems of Langston Hughes*. Edited by Arnold Rampersad. New York: Knopf, 1994.

Hunter, J. Paul. *The Norton Introduction to Poetry*. New York: W. W. Norton & Company, 1999.

Lear, Edward. *A Book of Limericks*. Boston: Little, Brown and Company, 1888.

Magill, Frank N., ed. *Cyclopedia of World Authors,* 3rd ed. Pasadena, CA: Salem Press, 1997.

Milton, John. *Paradise Lost and Paradise Regained*. Edited by Christopher Ricks. New York: New American Library, 1968.

Nash, Ogden. *The Adventures of Isabel*. Boston: Little, Brown, 1991.

Opie, Iona, and Peter Opie, eds. *The Oxford Book of Children's Verse*. Oxford: Oxford University Press, 1984.

Opie, Iona, and Peter Opie, eds. *The Oxford Dictionary of Nursery Rhymes*. Oxford: Clarendon Press, 1951.

Paz, Octavio. *Early Poems: 1935–1955*. Translated by Muriel Rukeyser et al. Bloomington: Indiana University Press, 1973.

Poe, Edgar Allan. *The Complete Poetry of Edgar Allan Poe*. New York: Signet Classic, 1996.

Rossetti, Christina. *The Complete Poems*. Edited by R. W. Crump. London: Penguin, 2001.

Sandburg, Carl. *The Complete Poems of Carl Sandburg,* rev. ed. New York: Harcourt Brace Jovanovich, 1970.

Schenck de Regniers, Beatrice, Eva Moore, and Mary Michaels White, eds. *Poems Children Will Sit Still For*. New York: Scholastic Book Services, 1969.

Shakespeare, William. *William Shakespeare: The Complete Works*. Edited by Alfred Harbage. New York: Viking, 1969.

Stephens, James, Edwin L. Beck, and Royall H. Snow, eds. *Victorian and Later English Poets*. New York: American Book Company, 1949.

Stevenson, Robert Louis. *A Child's Garden of Verses,* rev. ed. New York: Simon and Schuster Books for Young Readers, 1999.

Stringer, Jenny. *The Oxford Companion to Twentieth-Century Literature*. Oxford: Oxford University Press, 1996.

Trefethen, Florence. *Writing a Poem*. Boston: The Writer, Inc., 1975.

Untermeyer, Louis, ed. *A Galaxy of Verse*. New York: M. Evans and Company, Inc., 1978.

Untermeyer, Louis. *The Paths of Poetry: Twenty-Five Poets and Their Poems*. New York: Delacorte Press, 1966.

Various. *Contemporary Authors, New Revision Series*. Detroit: Gale Research Company, 1998.

Various. *Dictionary of Literary Biography*. Detroit: Gale Research Company, 1982.

Vinson, James, and D. L. Kirkpatrick. *Contemporary Poets*. New York: St. Martin's Press, 1985.

Weinberger, Eliot, ed. *The Collected Poems of Octavio Paz*. New York: New Directions Publishing Corp., 1987.

Whitman, Walt. *The Portable Walt Whitman*. Edited by Mark Van Doren. New York: Penguin, 1973.

CREDITS

AUDIO LISTING

All poems read by Anne Bobby and John Kolvenbach

Enjoy the rest of the Child's Introduction series!

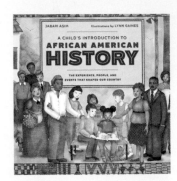

A Child's Introduction to African American History

A Child's Introduction to Art

A Child's Introduction to Ballet

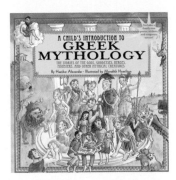

A Child's Introduction to Greek Mythology

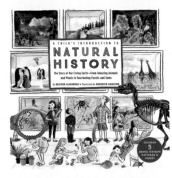

A Child's Introduction to Natural History

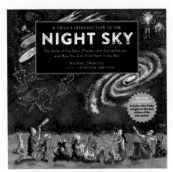

A Child's Introduction to the Night Sky

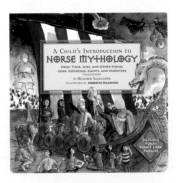

A Child's Introduction to Norse Mythology

A Child's Introduction to the Orchestra

A Child's Introduction to the World